My Asylum Days:

How Mental Health Policy Has Changed.

By

Dr Peter Carter OBE

impspired@gmail.com

Cover Art by Isabelle Masters

'The painting on the cover depicts a girl struggling with her mental health during Covid. The artist is the author's granddaughter, who did the painting as part of her Art GCSE.'

ISBN: 978-1-915819-86-4

This book is dedicated to all the people working with those who suffer from mental illness.

OTHER TITLES BY IMPSPIRED

Maybury –
by Mary Farrell

Polygon -
by Domonique

Leviathan –
by Jae Jenkins Scott

Hyperbola -
by Shelly Norris

Spun Tales and Woven Words –
by North Coast Writers

The Mining Muse –
by Marc Darnell

Apartmentalized –
by Dan Flore III

TABLE OF CONTENTS

About the Author

Dr Peter Carter OBE, PhD, MBA, FRCN, MCIPD, RCGP (Hon), ad eundem RCSI, RMN, RGN.

Peter Carter was CEO of the Royal College of Nursing from January 2007 to August 2015. Prior to that. He was CEO of the Central and Northwest London NHS Trust for twelve years. Peter is a registered mental health and adult nurse.

Peter is a graduate of the Institute of Personnel and Development and has a master's degree and PhD from the University of Birmingham. He is a Fellow of the Royal College of Nursing and an honorary fellow of the Royal College of General Practitioners, and an ed eundem of the Royal College of Surgeons of Ireland. In 2011 he was awarded the Inaugural Presidents Medal by the Royal College of Psychiatrists.

In 2006 he was awarded the O.B.E. by Her Majesty the Queen for his services to the NHS.

During his time at the RCN, Peter reshaped the organization and membership rose from 390,000 to 430,000. The college also achieved recognition in the *Sunday Times* top 100 companies to work for and achieved the gold award for *"Investors in people"*.

In 2010 he was a member of the Prime Ministers Commission on the Future of Nursing. He was also a member of the Crown Commission which devised the policy and protocols that led to the implementation of non-medical prescribing.

He is now an independent healthcare consultant. Since leaving the RCN he has worked across the U.K and internationally. He has on three occasions been asked by the NHS in England to be the interim Chair of NHS Trusts.

Peter has been the expert witness in over 200 cases of litigation in the health and social care systems. He has conducted investigations into serious acts of misconduct and serious untoward incidents. For example, Peter was a member of an investigation team into the homicide of a sex worker by a man who had a diagnosis of paranoid schizophrenia.

Whilst CEO of the Royal College of Nursing, Peter was regularly cited in the *Health Service journal* as one of the NHS's most influential people.

From 2010 to 2017 he was Honorary Colonel of 203 Field Hospital and went to Afghanistan and Iraq during the two conflicts.

He was a visiting Professor at Anglia Ruskin, Canterbury Christchurch and Kings College Universities. He is currently a visiting Professor at the University of Chester.

He has Honorary Doctorates from the Universities of Edge Hill, Bedfordshire, South Wales and Hertfordshire.

He has written articles in newspapers, professional journals and chapters in books.

He has participated in TV documentaries made many appearances on TV and radio. He has twice been the subject in the BBC programme *Hardtalk.*

PREFACE

Over the years I have shared anecdotes with friends and colleagues from the times that I worked in mental hospitals. My daughters Elizabeth and Catherine have encouraged me to put down in writing the stories that seemed to capture their attention and others who have heard them. Like many people I have talked about writing a book and now with their encouragement I have done it.

I have worked in six mental hospitals in different capacities over the years. Nowadays most mental hospitals have been closed or in a few cases reduced in size leaving only a few beds on what were massive sites often with their own farms creating a self-sufficient community. The Victorians built most and in their day they were progressive institutions heralding in a more enlightened approach to the care of what was then termed the Insane. Hitherto those suffering from mental health problems were demonised. It was generally held that "mad people were bad people" possessed by evil spirits and would be ostracised from society.

The Victorians built over 100 mental hospitals, known initially as "lunatic asylums". They literally took people out of the gutter or out of prisons and cared for them throughout their natural lives. Once in an asylum very few people were discharged. To be placed in an asylum people had to be "certified' which involved a physician or a magistrate deciding you were insane and signing a certificate to confirm this. Certification often meant a life sentence. The Victorians should not be criticised for this; far from it, they set a course that has been emulated worldwide and set in train a mind-set that changed society's view of insanity.

The downside was the failure of these institutions to move with the times. In the 1950s the drug chlorpromazine, commonly known as Largactil, transformed the prospects of people suffering from psychotic conditions such as schizophrenia. The hospitals failed to evolve from containment to therapy thus resulting in huge criticism from the late 1960's onwards.

The net effect of this was the massive closure programme that reached its pinnacle in the 1990's. The wholesale closure of mental hospitals was, in my view, a mistake. I believe there is a place for long-term care, call it an asylum, call it sanctuary, it doesn't matter. The closure programme has been too excessive and, by way of example, during 2015 there were a stream of concerns reported in the press over the shortage of beds. Many people were in prison who in previous eras would have been in mental health care. During Christmas 2014, a police officer in Devon was reduced to "tweeting" asking if there was a bed anywhere in the UK for a 14-year-old girl who was in a police cell when she should have been receiving care in a mental health facility.

There were accounts of patients in psychiatric units sleeping on the floor; of families in despair that they couldn't get a loved one admitted as there were no available beds; of people killing themselves in the absence of a responsive service; of psychiatrists at the end of their tether for the want of resources and politicians seemingly as lacking in insight as a person who is psychotic. The Victorians would be turning in their graves at this truly desperate state of affairs.

It therefore seems timely to give my account of the old mental hospitals that are so roundly condemned as being nothing other than cruel institutions. Everything I write is true. All I have done, with two exceptions, is to anonymise names of patients and staff. Even though many of those I cite, are long dead it doesn't seem right to identify these people, partly for fear of causing distress to relatives of the deceased and out of respect for those staff who were acting with good intentions even if at times they were misdirected.

Before describing my journey it is important to contextualise the mental hospitals and British society.

The 1960's

The 1960's are frequently described as the swinging 60's.

There is no doubt it was a decade of great change in British society. It was a decade that saw the acceleration of the end of the British Empire, which apart from the notable exceptions of the USA and Ireland had remained largely intact from its early beginnings in the 16th century until 1947 with the independence of India. There was increased momentum in the 1950's and then a virtual ending of Empire by the end of the 1960's.

Coupled with this, it was a decade of huge change within the UK. For example, the death penalty was abolished, homosexuality was decriminalised, abortions were legalised. The birch was abolished as a form of punishment for prisoners who broke rules. The breathalyser was introduced, dramatically reducing the death rate from alcohol-induced accidents eventually by eight-fold.

There was a shift from the age of deference.

This is personified by the Profumo affair in which a government minister was forced to resign, and the scandal was a contributory factor in the loss of the 1963 general election by the Conservative party. In earlier years the scandal would have been quietly hidden away as demonstrated by the conduct of high-profile people such as the wife of the Prime Minister Harold Macmillan who had a long-term affair with Lord Boothby who was a well-known hedonistic bi-sexual.

Empowerment of youth came to the forefront as can be seen by demonstrations against the Vietnam War, Mods and Rockers disrupting hitherto sedate Bank holiday weekends on the coast. With high employment, young people became important players in the consumer market, particularly in relation to clothes, entertainment, dining out, owning cars, scooters, motor bikes to mention but a few.

So what has this to do with mental hospitals?

In the 1960's, most of the care for people who were mentally ill was in mental hospitals.

When the Victorians built these hospitals they were usually in remote country areas and were largely self-sufficient. Their farms (both arable and livestock) ensured a plentiful supply of food; the "lunatics" as they were then called provided much of the labour.

The asylums were often the largest employers in the area where they were located as in addition to the physicians and attendants there were domestics, maintenance, farm workers, cooks etc.

There was very little oversight or regulation and people that were sent to the "Mad house" had long lengths of stay and were quickly institutionalised.

When I commenced my training as a psychiatric nurse in May 1968 I felt that I was stepping back in time. Although in the 1950's anti-psychotic drugs and anti-depressants drugs had revolutionised the treatment of people suffering from conditions such as schizophrenia, the regime for patients had changed little over the decades. The model of care was containment, rigid routines and uniformity of approach, irrespective of the needs of individual patients.

The dominant occupational group were the doctors followed by nurses. There were some occupational therapists, technical instructors such as carpenters and printers, involved in what was known as "industrial therapy", but the investment was minimal.

There was also an emergence of art and music therapy though this was very rare. Throughout the whole of the country there were 179 psychologists employed in mental hospitals, not even two to each hospital.

By 1960, the farms had nearly all closed and the fields were either fallow or subcontracted to local farmers. The hospitals were still self-contained in many other ways. There were staff social clubs where alcohol was inexpensive, sporting facilities for the staff were of the highest standards. Apart from the medical staff, most people were recruited locally with some from Ireland and. emerging in the 1960's, from Commonwealth countries. Mental hospitals also provided housing for the staff. Although the pay was low, the housing was subsidised, and the pension scheme for those with what was known as 'mental health officer status' enabled people to retire at the age of 55 with a pension nearly half of final salary index linked for life. Staff (mainly nurses) that were not married had accommodation free of charge as was food and laundry. There were cleaners that cleaned the rooms in staff residences, daily, in addition, there were a range of perks such as male nurses being provided with a two good quality tailor-made suits and three shirts every three years. It was common to find successive generations of families of staff employed and in many respects the hospitals were no different to the culture found in pit villages.

Job security was guaranteed. The staff enjoyed a comfortable and, in many respects, a working life free from the stress that others were experiencing in mainstream British life which could involve significant change in working practices as industries modernised and at times people were made redundant. These issues were not on the radar for mental hospital staff. The mind set was that you were in a job for life.

In that climate there was very little appetite for change.

Hildegard Peplau, a highly respected nurse and academic in 1989 gave an account of mental hospitals that describes the position perfectly.

The earliest model was hierarchical and more or less paternalistic. Many mental hospitals were in effect closed systems. They were self-contained villages, which, like old manor houses in Europe, were self-sustaining communities, presumably regulated in terms of 'good on the whole'.

Patients were the workers, attendants and nurses the patient custodial managers, while physicians prescribed treatments and in many instances the rules of conduct. The hospital staff for the most part lived within the compound and intermarriages (across levels of power and authority within the hospital) were common.

The people I met were mostly well meaning but had an inward-looking approach to their work and had little or no insight into their practice which, however well-intended, was institutional and at times punitive with little or no regard for the rights of the individuals.

In 1959 the government implemented a new Mental Health Act. Many staff viewed the new act as simply an increase in bureaucracy and form filling. It had been introduced as there was concern by the government because by 1955 the number of people in mental hospitals had soared to 150,000 and if left unchecked would have threatened the viability of the still fledgling NHS.

To stem the rising tide, it was anticipated that the new Mental Health Act would reduce the in-patient population with the introduction of the 'informal' patient. The Act implicitly condemned overcrowding as an organisational malpractice, productive in itself of a great deal of ill health. Peter Nolan, a highly respected nurse academic, commented in 1993 that the impetus for the Act was doubtless economic, but it also took account of and embodied the disaffection which had been mounting for years amongst those concerned with the plight of the mentally ill.

In 1968 I came across doctors and nurses who were trying to change things, but these were very much in the minority.

I had been interested in the work of a number of people who were writing about mental illness in a manner that was antagonistic to the then medical establishment. Psychiatrists, RD Laing, Thomas Szasz, David Cooper and Sociologist, Erving Goffman were highly prominent in what became known as the 'anti-psychiatry' movement. To my surprise, many of the staff I encountered working in mental health had either never heard of these people or if they had, were highly disparaging about them. This lack of dialogue was astonishing.

So too was the indifference to Enoch Powell's famous "Water Tower" speech who, when Minister of Health, stated at the annual conference of the National Association of Mental Health in 1961, that mental hospitals were part of a bygone age, and these 'doomed' institutions must disappear.

He stated:

This is a colossal undertaking, not so much in the new physical provision which it involves, as in the sheer inertia of mind and matter which it requires to overcome. There they stand, old-type asylums, isolated, majestic, imperious, brooded over by the gigantic water-tower and chimney combined, rising unmistakably and daunting out of the countryside -the asylums which our forefathers built with such immense solidity. Do not for one moment underestimate their powers of resistance to our assault. (Powell, 1961)

Powell's words were prophetic. The resistance to closure of these hospitals resulted in years of obfuscation and delay.

The way of life for the staff was such that the critical mass of staff in all disciplines had a vested interest in maintaining the status quo.

However, this inertia cannot be levelled simply at the door of the staff.

To transition from a model of care that had been largely unchanged for over 100 years required a change management programme. This did not happen. The change was engineered via a stream of policy initiatives, which had little or no buy-in from the staff and their representative bodies.

Historically there had been very little change in legislation relating to mental illness.

1808 to 1930

The key legislative milestones were:

1808 County Asylums Act.
1845 Lunacy Act.
1890 Lunacy Act.
1930 Mental treatment Act.

In 122 years there were four pieces of legislation but the basis of treatment and the managerial regime was largely unchanged over these years. It was another 30 years before there were any significant legislation or policy initiatives.

In parallel with these policy and legislative changes, there were a number of other factors that were to change the external perception of mental hospitals, which in turn had a huge impact on the provision of care and methods of working.

In August 1967, a nursing assistant wrote to the *News of the World* exposing the care of people in Ely Hospital, Cardiff. The allegations were of cruelty, verbal abuse, beatings, pilfering food, clothing and other items. There was an indifference to complaints particularly by the chief male nurse, lack of medical care, medication used to sedate patients, patients stripped and hosed down with cold water. Poor external scrutiny, out-of-touch senior management and incompetent local management were cited as the root causes of the failure to prevent or identify these problems.

Although Ely was a hospital for the mentally handicapped, (as what it was then termed) the findings sent shock waves throughout the world of mental health and learning difficulties. It sparked a series of inquiries into the care of people with mental illness and learning difficulties. It shattered the closed world of the mental hospitals and the Ely inquiry triggered a chain of reactions that not only were critical in kick-starting the demise of the hospitals but also impacted on the workforce that would change forever the closeted way of life they enjoyed.

Alongside the inquiries, the emerging anti –psychiatry phenomena gathered momentum.

The thinking of Laing, Cooper, Szasz and Goffman was belittled by mainstream conventional biological psychiatrists and many of those in other disciplines. Whilst the anti-psychiatry movement has nowadays been largely forgotten it nevertheless was an important ingredient in challenging the orthodox thinking of the day. Another significant development was the emergence of the organisation MIND.

Previously MIND was known as the National Association of Mental Health, the organisation where Enoch Powell had made his Water Tower speech at their annual conference in 1961.

This organisation developed into a highly influential pressure group that was effective at getting into the media their ideas on the change that was needed with a heavy emphasis on the closure of the mental hospitals. They were frequently at odds with the *Royal Medico-Psychological Association,* (now known as the *Royal College of Psychiatrists),* and nurses, who had a disparaging view of them, as MIND was frequently associated with being anti-nurse.

Nevertheless, they were effective. The 1980's were a watershed in terms of the momentum for closure. Although MIND was characterised as being a left- wing organization, they were bosom pals with the Thatcherite economists of the 80's who considered the hospitals to be expensive anachronisms sitting on real estate that could be sold off, thus releasing much needed capital in for the cash-strapped public purse.

Chapter 1: My beginning

It is the 26th May 1968 and I am eighteen years old. I'm sitting at the kitchen table in my home in Somerset. As I made my final preparations before leaving home, it was strange as I had mixed emotions. On one hand, excited at the prospect of the adventure facing me; on the other, saddened that this was a form of goodbye to my family and worried as to whether I would be able to make a success of my intention to train as a psychiatric nurse. My family had mixed feelings about my chosen career and many years later I can fully understand why. Some years after leaving home, my father gave me the book, *As I walked out one midsummer morning* by Laurie Lee. In the opening of the book Lee says, "As I left the house that chapter of my life closed for ever" This seems so apposite in relation to how I felt and now over 50 years later those sentiments are still with me as fresh today as they were then.

Home was a short walk to the railway station and as I said goodbye to my parents and left the house that chapter of my life truly did close forever.

Little did I know of how my life would change, the things I witnessed, the characters, the tragedies, the cruelty, the love, I could go on but rather than list the many events perhaps it's much better to explain them.

It was early on a Sunday evening that I arrived at the hospital. My instructions had been to report to reception and there a fellow student would take me to my living quarters. There were several different residences at the hospital, and I was allocated a room in the male nurse's hostel. This consisted of a 16-room facility of individual rooms and communal bath and toilet areas. The first thing that I became aware of was the cosmopolitan mix of my fellow students. There were people from Barbados, Mauritius, Malaysia, Nigeria plus people from different parts of the UK and Ireland. This was fascinating to me as Somerset had no ethnic minorities to speak of, coupled with my amazement that young people could travel from such far-flung parts of the world to work in, of all places, a mental hospital.

Most people in the UK had never visited their own asylums and, if they did, it was with fear and trepidation. I was quickly to discover that the entry ticket to the UK via a student visa was a prize worth seizing for many whose job prospects and career opportunities in their mother country were very limited. Of the many things I was to learn however is that, despite very different cultural backgrounds, there is far more that unites us than divides us. In fact, human nature, our wants and aspirations are very much the same irrespective of your origins.

The mental hospital world that I entered into was one of paradoxes and contradictions. The May 1968 intake that I was part of, was known as the PTS, "Preparatory Training School and "consisted of just four students, three women and myself. Two were from Malaysia and one from Hong Kong. A group this small was quite unusual and it felt strange as I found myself the minority ethnic member. Other PTS's could have up to twenty students.

The training school at the hospital had a very good reputation and I loved learning about psychiatry, the different illnesses, the history of mental illness, the treatments etc. Actually putting this into practice proved very difficult.

MY FIRST WARD PLACEMENT

After the 6-week introductory training block which was almost all class-room based, the training over three years, consisted of a series of ward and clinical placements of three months each interspersed with two-week study periods in the School of Nursing. At the eighteen-month stage of training, there was a three-hour written exam set by the then General Council for Nursing (GNC). At the end of the course there was another three-hour exam, a viva with a nurse tutor and a consultant psychiatrist, and a practical assessment.

Overall, mental hospitals were unintentionally punitive. Patients were suppressed and containment was the order of the day. Although, as a result of the anti-psychotic medication that had emerged in the 1950's, mental hospitals were much more open, they were overall, with a few exceptions, spartan places. I had also not realised that there would be such a high proportion of elderly patients. Hospitals were segregated into male and female sides. Geriatric wards on the male side of the hospital were, in most cases, truly awful and had my first placement been in one I think I would have walked away.

More of that later.

My first ward allocation was to what in mental hospital parlance was a "back ward". These were wards full of people who had been in hospital for most of their adult lives. Many had a diagnosis of schizophrenia or what was then termed, manic depression. I was so fortunate that this was my first ward. The charge nurse, John, was a highly experienced man who was coming to the end of his career. I learnt so much from him in those first three months. He was compassionate, thoughtful and had a progressive approach to his work. The patients were fascinating. Some had been in the hospital for 60 years and although in most cases their schizophrenia had burnt out or their manic depressive cycles had diminished, the ravages of spending so much time incarcerated in an asylum had, to all effects, driven the individuals mad. That may appear to be an incongruous statement as most lay people would assume the "madness" came first. Not so. It is now well understood that even those with a severe mental health problems can function well if provided with adequate support and treatment. Far too often, the impact of spending years in a mental hospital was as damaging as the original illness.

The atmosphere on the ward was as depicted in many movies such as *One flew over the Cuckoo's nest*. One man constantly walking around telling everyone that he had a clean bum. This man had been a conscientious objector in the Second World War. On studying his case notes, I learnt that he had been a post-office clerk with no apparent signs of mental illness. He was a devout Quaker and had refused to be conscripted at the outbreak of war. As a result, he was prosecuted, judged to be insane and was sent to a mental hospital where, from reading his case notes, he was subjected to ridicule and scorn from both staff and fellow patients. The charge nurse confirmed that, like many others, it was the hospital itself that had caused the man to have been driven mad rather than his illness. The charge nurse also explained to me that, in the confusion and chaos in Britain at the outset of war, some conscientious objectors were actually forced to work in mental hospitals thus releasing the staff to go and fight, as was the case with this charge nurse, whilst others were certified. So much depended on the vagaries of the magistrate.

There were others such as Harry who was 88-years-old and had been admitted in 1900. The beautifully transcribed copper plate writing in his case notes described how he was brought to the hospital in a horse and trap. He was diagnosed as suffering from dementia praecox, the forerunner of schizophrenia. He was also educated at one of Britain's pre-eminent public schools and although, from his notes, in the first few decades of his stay in hospital he received visitors, he had lost contact with his family some 40 years earlier. A lost soul who sat looking endlessly into space.

Patient after patient fascinated me but also so did the staff, some of whom were as institutionalised as the patients in their own self-contained world. This was 1968, the decade of liberalism and so-called progression, but it felt like the 1930's. This even applied to so many of the younger staff who quickly became subsumed by the way of life.

One patient in particular was a source of interest of me. He was nicknamed by the staff as "The Duke" and he too had been in the hospital for many years. He was fourteen when admitted in 1918. Although now 64 years old, he was fit and active and could easily have passed for 50. In speaking with him, he did not appear to have had any sign of mental illness although he had a diagnosis of delusions of grandeur. He insisted that he was the son and heir of one of the country's landed gentry, hence the nickname the Duke. It was interesting that he looked distinguished and, unlike so many other patients, the years of incarceration did not appear to have taken its toll on him although I noticed, whenever we went for walks outside the hospital grounds, he became silent and withdrawn, totally lacking in confidence, hardly surprising.

He worked in the hospital's garden department and, like all of Britain's mental hospitals, the grounds and gardens were resplendent and why wouldn't they be with a feudal system of a never-ending supply of cheap labour. The grounds were manicured to perfection.

However, on a fine June afternoon with the sunshine and the grounds of the hospital looking their best, we received a phone call from the hospital reception say that Harold aka "The Duke" had a visitor. The charge nurse was taken aback as in all his years he never knew him to have a visitor. The only thing known about his family was that he was born to a girl who was 15 years old and he had been taken away from her at birth. The whereabouts of the mother was unknown and Harold had been brought up in an orphanage. The reason he had been sent to the hospital was that he had been telling all and sundry that he was the heir to one of the country's titled families. Although I am writing this in 2024, I am not revealing the name of the family to whom he says he was related, as even now, I fear it would cause controversy and would serve no good purpose.

I went to the hospital reception to accompany the visitor to the ward. The man I met was distinguished-looking in his late 50s, he was well- dressed and clearly a person of substance. He had a firm confident hand- shake accompanied by a trans-Atlantic accent which, on enquiry, turned out to be Canadian. On arrival at the ward, I introduced him to the charge nurse and I was despatched to find Harold who was working in the hospital grounds. When I explained to Harold (I never referred to him as The Duke) that he had a visitor, he almost went into a state of shock, "Me a visitor, are you sure?" It was at that point I could see the likeness between Harold and our mysterious visitor from Canada. On arrival back at the ward the charge nurse introduced Harold to his brother.

"Brother I have a brother?" "Yes you do". Whilst I had been out locating Harold our Canadian visitor had explained the following.

Harold's mother was in service to a wealthy titled family and had become pregnant at the age of fifteen, the father allegedly being one of the teenage sons of the then Duke. To avoid a scandal, the baby had been taken away at birth and Harold's mother has been despatched by boat to Canada to work in service to a relative of the Duke. Harold's mother had eventually married and her husband had become a successful businessman. She had several children all of whom had equally become successful in various businesses or professional ventures, law etc. She had nursed her secret all her life and had always felt guilt and remorse over her lost son and hardly a day had passed in her long life when she had not thought of him. She made several unsuccessful attempts to locate the son who had been taken away from her at birth. Harold's mother had died in 1966 but had told her family of these events in the last year of her life.

As a result, her son in Canada embarked on a quest to locate Harold which had resulted in him arriving at the hospital. It transpired that, even in the 1960's, (via public records) tracing people via public records was not actually that difficult. Having located his brother he travelled to England but had chosen not to announce his visit beforehand in case the forewarning may have had some form of deleterious effect on Harold, when the brother realised he had been in hospital since the age of 14.

Well this, as you might imagine, really opened up Pandora's Box, Harold was triumphant: "I told you all but you wouldn't believe me" and so on. This then created a conundrum. What to do? All of the main players in this saga were long dead and the scarring of Harold due to his lifelong stay in an asylum meant that any sense of public exoneration was pointless and possibly very destructive.

Over the next few weeks Harold's brother visited daily and took him out for long drives in a hired car. A case conference was convened with the upshot that all agreed the years of institutionalisation rendered Harold incapable of re-joining society. Harold's brother made a substantial financial arrangement so that his brother would want for nothing; clothes from high street shops, cigarettes, and confectionary were no object. At the case conference, his brother raised the issue of the years of ridicule and said that he would not be formally complaining but that from now on the nickname "Duke" should be dropped and that his brother should be afforded the respect that he warranted. His brother promised to return from Canada and in the interim period he would keep in touch. Tragically, three months after the visit Harold was found dead in his bed by member of the night staff. He had suffered a massive heart attack and died peacefully in his sleep. The only mystery is how Harold had known about his past.

Having been separated from his mother at birth and brought up in an orphanage, it must be assumed that a member of staff told him of his antecedents, hence setting off a chain of events that resulted in him being certified and kept in a mental hospital throughout his adult life. There are countless stories of this nature some of which I will dilate upon later in this book.

THE HOSTEL

As I have already mentioned, the hostel I lived in consisted of 16 young men all of whom were training to be psychiatric nurses. I was to meet a number of characters who made a big impression on me in both a positive and negative way. There was something odd about the way in which people conducted themselves in this cloistered environment. Some of the antics are so extreme that I hesitate to write about them as the reader may consider them to be too far-fetched and that the passing years may have caused me to exaggerate or embellish the various antics. This is not the case. I remember the events as clearly today as when I lived through them over 50 years ago.

We used to sit in a common room often talking for hours. Politics, sport, and girls; the list is endless. One of the most interesting characters was a guy whose nickname was Malteser. Not sure why he had this nickname, but he was one of the most likeable yet most irresponsible people I had ever met and to this day I do not believe I have ever met anyone quite like him. He was loud, intelligent, immodest, and sensitive in many respects but at times bad news to be with. I once went to the cinema with him. We were sitting towards the back and just before the lights went down he spotted two young women: "Oh look there's Liz and Jane" and he hurriedly raced down the aisle, went along the empty row behind them, and simultaneously and placing his head between theirs shouted "boo", and gave both a kiss on their cheeks. To his horror both the startled young women looked at him in a state of shock and it was at that moment he realised it was a case of mistaken identity. The lights had gone down as he exited from the cinema, the two offended individuals got to their feet and a commotion ensued with the usherette leading them to the back of the cinema whilst the manager was summoned. I sat there petrified for fear of being implicated. The police arrived and the rows were scanned by the police, the ushers and by the two women but to no avail. I certainly did not enjoy the film but decided to sit it out as leaving early might have pointed the finger at me.

On arriving back at the hostel, Malteser was in a relaxed frame of mind having regaled those present with his exploits of that evening. Anyone else would have maintained their silence, but not Malteser who traded off it.

On another occasion, one afternoon we were watching a TV documentary on the 1956 Hungarian uprising. it was topical, as the Dubcek Prague spring of 1968 had just been put down by the Russians. During the documentary much was made of the fact that the Hungarians' principal weapon was Molotov cocktails. A debate ensued among us as to how Molotov cocktails were made. "Oh, it's simple" said Malteser. "All you do is fill a bottle with petrol, bung a petrol-soaked rag into it, set fire to it and throw it." This was disputed by a Scotsman called Ben, a giant of a man who said that the bottle should not be filled to the top. To cut a long story short, Malteser said he would make one and demonstrate. A milk bottle was retrieved from the kitchen along with a drying up towel. The petrol was obtained by disconnecting the fuel line from the motorcycle of an anorak student nurse called William. Adjacent to the hostel was a large building that housed garden machinery used in the hospital grounds. Malteser assured everyone that no damage would be done as the bottle, when thrown against the wall, would simply smash and the petrol would ignite and quickly burn itself out with no damage to the wall. This would have been the case had Malteser not thrown the bottle too high against the wall which meant the petrol went up to the eaves and promptly set fire to some dry grass in the guttering. Exit quick left by most of the audience. Malteser, quick as a flash, ran into the hostel and emerged with a fire hose and began to douse the fire. The head gardener happened by and shouted "What's going on?" Malteser, whilst still at work, shouted that he had spotted the fire from the hostel television lounge. "Good work" shouted the head gardener who activated the hospital's fire alarm system. By the time the fire brigade arrived, the fire had been extinguished and, astonishingly, they accepted his explanation. It was decided that, being a hot period, somehow dry grass in the guttering had ignited. Then, to top it all, the hospital management committee decided at its next meeting to award Malteser a certificate and book token for his prompt action. We were all invited to attend a small ceremony when he was given his award. He was on a placement in the occupational therapy department at the time where he made a frame in the woodwork department and then hung it in his room in the hostel. When visiting his room, we would put it to him that surely, he felt a fraud, as it was he who started the fire. Incredibly he said that wasn't the point. The certificate was for his prompt action in putting the fire out; the fact that he had started it seemed completely lost on him. Incorrigible, likeable, insufferable! As a psychiatric nurse he was brilliant, kind, insightful, tolerant. He never finished his training. He left to join the army where I understand he had a successful career.

Some of the other characters

My colleagues in the hostel all differed. Some were highly intelligent but lacking in direction, others were flawed in many ways, drifting from job to job, with very few having an obvious vocation for nursing. But because we were so diverse, we had lively discussions about politics, sport, law and order, and any contentious news that could arouse contrary opinions.

Because of the nature of the work, some of them had gradually become case-hardened, and highly descriptive accounts of the day's work were the norm.

I met fellow students who had been in the armed forces, others who were clearly very bright but had dropped out of school and had not completed their education and, in turn, failing (so far) to realise their potential.

The salaries for student nurses were low, although the accommodation, food and laundry were all free. Consequently, some of us had part time-jobs to supplement our income. Many of us worked as cleaners in a local school which virtually doubled our income.

The hospital had a social club and, as there were no rates or utility bills, the alcohol was much cheaper than in local pubs. In addition, most mental hospitals had married accommodation for staff, often two- and three-bedroom houses that would normally be out of the price range of nursing staff. The downside of this was that mental hospitals often became closed communities, hence the sense that some staff became as institutionalised as the patients. It was this phenomenon that did so much to impede progress in moving away from an outmoded model of care and into the new world of community-based services geared up to not only keeping people out of hospital but also to ensuring a much more therapeutic environment helping people to recover from breakdowns and other forms of mental illness.

And so I had embarked on my training. As I said the first ward was just right for me, a progressive charge nurse who instilled some of the core principles that were to stand me in good stead for the challenges to come.

Chapter 2: My second ward placement

My next ward placement was on a male geriatric ward. There were 45 patients and four staff. The conditions were truly appalling. The patients were a mixture of those who had suffered from mental illness all their lives and had grown old in the hospital and others who had developed Alzheimer's and other forms of dementia later in life and could not be cared for by their families. It was interesting to reflect on this mixture. On one hand, people who had been in the hospital for 50 to 60 years and had a diagnosis of schizophrenia, manic depression, psychopathy, OCD and so on, coalescing with people who may have been very successful in their professional lives such as lawyers, businessmen, accountants who, because of the way in which their dementia manifested itself, were unmanageable. This was particularly the case in the hospital I trained at as it was in a highly affluent area, hence many of the patients coming from professional backgrounds. These people could become aggressive, doubly incontinent, wandering off thus rendering their families unable to cope.

The effect of this made life very difficult. Families often had very understandable expectations of a higher standard of care and were frequently shocked at the conditions their loved ones were in. Whereas the patients that had grown old in the hospital rarely if ever had visitors.

To demonstrate the difference among the patients I will give five brief case studies.

STANLEY

Stanley was in his seventies and had been in the hospital since his early twenties. He originally had a diagnosis of paranoid schizophrenia and had a long history of extreme violence and aberrant behaviour. He had spent most of his life on what was known as the refractory ward. This was the ward where the most violent and disturbed patients were nursed.

Now in his seventies, he was ill with bowel cancer and, although far less physically powerful than he had been, he was still strong and remained aggressive. He was kept locked in a room of his own. This was because he was prone to strike out and could easily have inflicted serious harm to many of the other patients most of whom were elderly and frail. In addition, because of his mental state he would eat his own faeces. This coupled with the bowel cancer meant that he had lost bowel control and would frequently take his clothes off and defecate on the floor and then proceed to eat the faeces. As a consequence of his schizophrenia, he had echolalia, which meant that whenever spoken to, he would repeat what had been said to him. Apart from the echolalia, the only other thing he would say was to announce his name: "I'm Stanley Harry Pullen so sod off" which could go on for hours. The cancer was not treated, as it was impossible for him to be examined without several nurses holding him down. Therefore any notion of surgery was out of the question. It was our job each morning to go into his room masked and gloved to clean him up and to clean the room. How he survived was beyond me. He lived for several years in this state.

DONALD

Donald's case is one of the saddest I have ever encountered. He was an airline pilot who in his spare time was a keen cyclist. There was no history of mental illness in the family and he was happily married with two young children. One day whilst out cycling he was involved in a road accident resulting in severe brain damage and confining him to a wheelchair. As a result of his brain injury he was prone to severe outbursts of violence often brought on through the frustrations of being in a wheelchair and, despite the injury, retaining sufficient insight to recall his previous life and now living with significant intellectual impairment.

Although only in his late forties, he was on a geriatric ward as his verbal outbursts could have rendered him vulnerable to other patients who would not have tolerated his abuse. In addition, the geriatric ward was better equipped for wheelchair-bound patients. Donald would become distressed and upset frequently screaming, "I'm stuck in this hole, this is a right hole"

His wife visited regularly but never brought the children as it would have been too distressing. When Donald's wife arrived at the ward his face would light up and she would spend hours talking with him, wheeling him round the hospital grounds and would bath and shave him. However, when the time came to leave Donald would plead with her to take him home which was of course unrealistic due to his unpredictability. Both Donald and his wife would weep. It was so upsetting and the staff felt for them. After his wife had left, Donald would either continue to weep or become aggressive thus resulting in him being kept in a separate room. He too lived for many years, but with the passing of time his outbursts lessened although he was never well enough to leave the hospital.

GREGORY

Gregory had manic depression and had been in and out of hospital most of his adult life. Now in his seventies, he developed a degenerative muscular condition, that confined him to a wheelchair. The cycles of manic depression had long passed but, because of his condition, he was unable to care for himself and had no living relatives. In 1968, there simply were no facilities to assist someone of Gregory's disposition. He was fun to be with and liked a cuddle from the female nurses when they put him to bed. Unfortunately, Gregory could at times become aggressive. However, because of his physical condition he didn't really pose a threat apart from one aspect. Despite his muscular condition he had a vice like grip. If he was in a temper he would await a passing patient to go by and would grab whatever part of their body he could and inflict serious pain until the nursing staff prised him away. The remedy was to place Gregory in a part of the ward where couldn't make physical contact with anyone until he had calmed down. Afterwards he was remorseful although the staff were always careful to suss him out before a good night cuddle. The most notorious event with Gregory was during a visit by the hospital management committee. One member of the committee was a vicar. During the visit Gregory spotted the clerical collar and beckoned the vicar over to him. The vicar obliged and Gregory spoke very quietly thus making the vicar bend down to hear, once within range Gregory proceeded to wrap both hands around the vicar's throat. In the ensuing melee, both the vicar and Gregory ended up on the floor and it took two of us to prise them apart.

Unfortunately Gregory had seriously damaged the vicar's throat and an ambulance was called to take him to the local general hospital. The vicar was left with permanent damage to his vocal chords and swallowing mechanism. In addition he was significantly traumatised. Gregory explained that he didn't like vicars.

ERIC AND KENNETH KENDALL

Kenneth Kendall was a broadcaster who worked as a newsreader for the BBC for many years.

Eric was in his eighties and had been in hospital most of his adult life. He suffered from schizophrenia and despite his advancing years was still active and could become highly animated to the point of disturbing other patients. One of the things that could spark him off was when Kenneth Kendall was reading the evening news on TV. As soon as Eric saw that it was Kendall he would start shouting telling him to get out of the ward accusing him of coming in and stealing from him. This in turn would set other patients off some of whom would say things such as "you're mad and should be locked up" or others would then respond by saying things such as "he is mad and is locked up" within a few moments the ward could be in a state of chaos. We quickly learnt that as soon as the news came on and it was Kenneth Kendall one of us would sprint over and turn to another TV channel.

Eric would be upset for a while and would then settle down. Why Kenneth Kendall, who knows?

FREDDIE

Freddie was an interesting character. He had been a merchant seaman for all of his working life. Consequently, he spent long periods at sea. There was no history of mental illness in his family and, to all intent and purposes, he lived a normal life. In his sixties, he became depressed and suffered from mood swings. As his condition deteriorated, he was eventually referred to a psychiatrist and was admitted to hospital as he was deemed a suicide risk due to his depression. As part of the assessment process, blood tests were carried out and it emerged that Freddie had syphilis. The effect of this was that he was suffering from general paralysis of the insane, commonly known as GPI. Nowadays this condition is rarely heard of, at its height, it accounted for 20% of people who were in mental hospitals. Basically, the bacterium *Treponema pallidum* causes lesions throughout the body including the brain. This disease was virtually eradicated in the west following the discovery of penicillin. It was therefore an unusual case.

Freddie was bedbound and covered in pressure sores. Most were gangrenous and he was covered in dressings and in great pain. Despite this, he was optimistic and even on the morning he died he ate a bowl of porridge. His physical state was so poor that huge areas of skin would detach from his body. One particular day, whilst we were attending to him, most of the skin on his back came away. My colleague Paul was physically sick at the sight of it. I didn't feel too good about it. Freddie was the first body I laid out. The charge nurse, Tom showed me how to do it. The dignity afforded to Freddie was heart-rending and Tom dressed all the wounds as if Freddie was still alive. It was another of those building blocks for me. Tom talked about respect for the deceased.

The remainder of the patients were, in most cases, harmless and were vulnerable as opposed to in any way presenting a threat.

The routine was set and never changed. Each morning every patient had to be out of bed and dressed. The dress code was heavy-duty two-piece suits, shirts and ties, leather shoes and thick woollen socks. I make reference to this as the clothing was hard-wearing and designed to last. It was uncomfortable and, particularly in hot weather, unbearable. As many of the patients were incontinent, there was a constant round of changing and washing them throughout the shift. Patients were often distressed and resistive to being changed. This, coupled with the faeces and urine, rendered the job as unpleasant as you can imagine. Additionally, as many of the patients were in chairs that had a table across them thus rendering them unable to stand up, many had developed pressure sores that were gangrenous. These sores would have been very painful, gave off an unpleasant odour and were untreatable. I became used to seeing full thickness sores exposing bone.

How I and others stayed is beyond me. Washing, bathing, changing, feeding was a never-ending cycle.

The charge nurse, Tom, was an Irishman who I really liked. He was jovial, kind and had a great work ethic. Like many Irish people I was to work with, Tom was articulate, thoughtful and had a pragmatic approach to life. I admired his vocabulary which he put down to a Christian Brothers education and he was particularly adept at helping relatives come to terms with the awful reality that their loved ones found themselves in during the last few years of their lives.

Of the many memories that I have of Tom, two in particular come to mind.

The first was an incident about six weeks into my three-month placement on the ward.

Each morning, after we had got the patients out of bed and after their breakfast, the staff would have a cup of tea. The tea was taken in the ward area as it would not have been practical for purposes of observation or if an aggressive outburst occurred if some of us were in the staff room. One of the nurses, Brenda, was a middle-aged woman who was a bundle of energy and enthusiasm. She loved the patients and was a model of care and compassion. I was to work out later in life that this was her way of coping. She never reflected on the appalling standards of the ward which was far too big, overcrowded and understaffed, quite apart from the stench and the nature of the work.

On a particular morning as we sat there, me quiet, a nursing assistant deep in her thoughts, Tom serving the tea and Brenda a picture of happiness and contentment humming away, Tom noticed that I was surveying this scene of human carnage and suffering. Tom inquired, in that lovely Irish way, "a penny for your thoughts Peter". I replied "A penny for my thoughts Tom. If something is not done about these appalling conditions and the way these people are suffering, it would be better if they all passed away and they were out of their misery".

At this, Brenda erupted, was crying and genuinely distraught. I tried to reassure her that all I was saying was that the conditions were awful, and I was concerned about the standards of care. Brenda in her distressed state said that we look after the "babies" nicely and that what I said was "horrible". Flo, the nursing assistant, had swiftly moved away and clearly wanted nothing to do with this. Tom eventually calmed Brenda and asked me to apologise which I did. He later counselled me to keep those thoughts to myself as, whilst he understood my sentiments, I would get myself a bad name by speaking in such a manner.

My second memory was an incident that involved what I would describe as an upper middle-class family who were very difficult and demanding. I could understand their concerns because, as I have demonstrated, the conditions were appalling. The trouble with the family is that they directed their anger, frustration and guilt at the front-line staff.

Nothing ever went right. They complained about everything and Tom was a model of patience and tolerance in listening to their issues and helping to calm troubled waters.

However, on a particular day, they overstepped the mark and I saw a side of Tom that I did not think existed.

Adjacent to the hospital was another large hospital for what was then called the mentally sub-normal. To help supplement the shortage of staff, some patients from that hospital helped out on the geriatric wards. These were people of low IQ who really didn't need to be in hospital and were a valuable addition to the team. We had Michael who used to turn up four times a week. He was kind and showed great empathy for the patients. He and I got on really well and he told me that his parents were very old when they had him and both had died when he was young and, as there was no-one else to look after him, he had been put into the hospital when he was ten years old. Now in his early twenties he was happy in his world and enjoyed coming over the road to the hospital to help out.

One day when the wife and adult children of the middle-class family were visiting, they noticed that their loved one had odd-coloured socks on, one blue, and one brown. Instead of simply asking for the socks to be changed, they blew up and used expressions such as "so you people can't even put the same colour socks on him". It went on with Brenda trying to calm them. Tom emerged and, after establishing the nature of the latest problem, asked Michael to go to the patient's locker and bring another pair of socks. A few moments later, Michael standing in the doorway of the dormitory called to Tom, who was still trying to appease the relatives, that he could not change the socks. A quizzical Tom asked why. Michael replied that, because the other pair were also blue and brown, and held the two socks up to demonstrate the point.

Before Tom had the chance to respond, the wife bellowed out to Michael that he was a stupid imbecile and proceeded to traduce him further until Tom intervened. Without raising his voice, but with a steely determination, Tom put it to them that the root cause of their disaffection was the guilt they felt at putting their relative in a mental hospital and whilst this was understandable to a point, their conduct was indefensible and that Michael was a human being with feelings. Tom added that Michael was someone who had shown her husband untold acts of kindness: giving him drinks, soothing him when he was disturbed, changing him when incontinent and so on. Tom then said that, if they did not apologise to Michael, they would have to take their relative home with them as Tom would refuse to allow his staff to be subjected to such abuse.

We and the relatives were taken aback at this. Almost

instantly an apology was given to Michael and from that moment onwards the relatives came to terms with the fact that, whilst the conditions were as bad as you could imagine, taking it out on the front-line staff was not the solution. Of the many things I learned from Tom was that you could confront things without being aggressive as this only exacerbates the situation.

At the end of my three months I thanked Tom for his wisdom and guidance. Brenda and I were on quiet but cordial terms whist Flo the nursing assistant kept her own counsel but did kiss me goodbye. Tom said it had been a pleasure having me on his ward and said that I was a good nurse. I truly valued that compliment.

I sometimes think of them and wondered what became of Michael.

Chapter 3: The locked ward

After the three months on the geriatric ward there couldn't have been a bigger contrast with the locked ward of the hospital.

The ward was well-staffed, with 40 patients and six staff on duty, which included two student nurses.

The regime was strict and was geared to minimise aggression.

Patients were never left unsupervised. There was no free access to bathrooms and the lavatories did not have locks on the doors. Patients were shaved by the staff using electric razors. Two razors for forty patients and this was a job delegated to student nurses. Medication was the principal treatment and whilst patients were not doped up in the way often described as the "chemical cosh", the prescriptions were at the higher end of the scale but always within the recommended limits. Knives and forks were counted out at the beginning and end of every meal and patients were not allowed to leave the dining room tables until all the cutlery was accounted for.

Patients that were in a disturbed state could be confined to a locked side room or, if significantly violent or prone to self-harm, to the padded cell.

At the end of the afternoon shift, all patients were in bed prior to the night staff coming on duty. A few worked with the staff, sweeping and cleaning the ward in readiness for the next day. This meant patients getting into their pyjamas at 8pm even on hot summer days. On coming on duty, the night staff commenced a drug round with most patients being on some form of night sedation. A number of patients were addicted to the drug paraldehyde, which was a very strong sedative. Everything was done to minimise the risk of violence. The dormitory was communal with not even curtains by each bed to afford some form of privacy. At the end of the ward dormitory were six side rooms where some patients were locked in for the night. These were usually patients that could cause problems. For example, one man was a prolific pilferer and would take tobacco from patients' lockers. Tobacco was valuable currency. Most patients smoked and losing your tobacco was a cause of conflict usually resulting in violence. Others had a history of disinhibited sexual behaviour and were not averse to sexually interfering with other patients, again a source of conflict if the advances were not welcomed.

The patients were an eclectic group: psychopaths, schizophrenics, Munchausen's syndrome, manic-depressives, alcoholics, people who were a suicide risk. The people who were at risk of suicide were always particularly interesting: often with no pre-existing mental illness who had attempted suicide because of a failed business, financial worries or relationship problems.

One particular man comes to mind who had tried to kill himself because he thought he was at risk of abusing children. This was one of the saddest cases I had ever come across. The fact was that he had never done so but felt he could not live with himself. I played chess with him on a number of occasions. The charge nurse advised me not to raise the subject with him and that the more he could engage in "normal" pursuits without reference to his fears, the better the chance of him resolving the issue and moving forward. In many respects this suited me. I was eighteen and would have felt out of my depth. One day during chess, he asked me why he thought he might do it. I replied that I really had no idea but that he was a good, decent man and that I hoped he would overcome his fantasies and resume a life outside of the hospital. He thanked me for my comments and gave me a brief smile. I thought his appreciation of my comments were undoubtedly genuine though his smile was one of resignation.

Many months later, he managed to abscond from the ward and killed himself by standing in front of an express train. The fact that his method of suicide was so brutal signified to me that he wanted to smash himself out of this world and that there was no turning back. Over the subsequent years, I worked with many people who eventually killed themselves or attempted to do so. Some people go to bed full of alcohol and drugs never to wake up again: others asphyxiate themselves; some cut their wrists or their throats. Train suicides are common, with people laying across the track. However to stand full on with your arms open watching a train hurtle before you signifies the depth of the need to ensure there is no turning back. Quite aside from my sympathy for the individual, my thoughts on these occasions are also with the train driver and of course the relatives of the deceased. By dying in this way identification of the body is very difficult. Many years after this event, I went with a colleague to a morgue to identify a patient who had killed himself in the same way. All we could see was part of a face that had remained intact, his body parts had been strewn over several hundred yards as the train came to a halt and were in a crumpled pile on the viewing table. Therefore, for the family there would be no goodbye in an undertaker's premises or a chapel of rest. No chance for a last goodbye holding a hand or as some people do a kiss and an embrace. A sad and tragic end to a life.

Occasionally there were patients whom the staff suspected of feigning mental illness as a way of exculpating themselves from facing criminal charges after committing a crime. One man in particular had been involved in serious financial fraud but had managed to convince psychiatrists and the courts that he was mentally ill.

Wards had two charge nurses, one for each shift, and I thought I was fortunate to be allocated to the shift that was headed by another Irish charge nurse, Thomas. He again was really well read and was a great conversationalist. He was always ready to answer questions and was an excellent tutor, coach and mentor, not that he would have ever described himself in those terms.

Attached to the ward was a building that provided therapy for patients, known as factories. This therapy consisted of patients carrying out repetitive tasks. The hospital had won contracts with local companies and involved labour-intensive tasks such as packing items into boxes. One contract was for aftershave. The company was very generous in giving free samples to the staff. The quality was not of the highest but at least the staff and patients all smelt the same.

Another contract was for assembling toy guns. These were the little derringers made famous in the cowboy series "Maverick". Thousands of guns were assembled each year and were exported all over the world. The task involved taking the precast body of the gun and inserting the trigger mechanism and attaching, using small hammers, the plastic covering of the handles and then packing them in a presentation box with some bullets.

The patients were paid a modest amount for this work. Many people might hold the view that this type of "therapy" would not have any benefit and initially so did I. In fact, this was not the case. The therapy provided a welcome distraction from the drudge of being incarcerated in the locked ward. And whilst the unit was locked, many of the patients enjoyed the work. Only patients who were not in a disturbed state were allowed into the factory and therefore the atmosphere was relaxed. Tea was readily available and the radio provided a musical accompaniment to the work.

As with the geriatric ward, the mix of patients was interesting. Some had been in the hospital for most of their adult lives, whilst others as described above had no previous contact with mental health services.

It was on this ward that I first witnessed extreme outbursts of violence and anger. For example, one morning during breakfast a man who was an alcoholic and was admitted against his will for detox pushed his way through the queue at the breakfast hatch. A patient who had been remote and unresponsive exploded with anger, grabbing the large metal teapot from the nurse who was dispensing tea and smashed it into the face of the alcoholic who fell to the ground and was then subjected to a ferocious beating around the head. The incident took just a few seconds before the nurses intervened but by then the man had sustained significant injuries.

This incident not only shocked me but gave me a new perspective to the work. Until that incident, I thought the man who reacted so violently was a passive individual and I really couldn't understand why he was in a locked ward.

Thomas the charge nurse explained that although now in his late sixties, the patient was physically very strong. This was compounded as he had what was known in the sub-culture of mental hospitals as an "an epileptic personality"

The man had severe epilepsy and, despite heavy anti-convulsant drugs, still had major fits. These were known as grand mal seizures. They often came on without warning and a cursory look at someone who suffered from grand mals revealed that their faces were covered with scars from the injuries sustained over many years from falling. In addition, if a patient when having a fit was in an area of the ward where the staff were not present, the long-stay patients would take the opportunity of going through their pockets and taking their tobacco or anything else such as confectionery. In the post-fit period known as a fugue the first thing an epileptic would do, even in their confused state, would be to check their pockets to see if they had been pilfered. Little wonder then that they spent as much time as possible sitting on chairs near the nurses and little wonder that they had a resentful and suspicious personality. Most people, including the staff, kept away from them as they were so touchy and suspicious and only really made contact when there was a need such as for the administration of medication. Interestingly, despite their undoubted problems, these people understood the need for anti-convulsant drugs and were not at all difficult when it came to taking their medication.

The concept of an 'epileptic personality' is one that I refute. It was the effects of the institution combined with the epilepsy that, never knowing when the next fit was coming, and being so vulnerable, resulted in their disposition.

There are countless interesting case studies that I could go into.

Here are a few other patient profiles that the reader may find of interest.

There was a patient with Munchausen's syndrome. This

man was fascinating. He purported to be an Australian spitfire pilot and was extremely plausible. He was, in fact, a confidence trickster. He regularly got himself admitted to general hospitals feigning illness. He did it really well and would often be in hospital for long periods of time whilst his symptoms were investigated. As soon as it became clear to the clinicians that he was a fraud, he would simply up and go, usually to the next town where the cycle would start again. Eventually he became quite notorious and the remedy was to section him under the Mental Health Act. He had been in the hospital for many years. There was no plan and no therapy, simply containment. One day after many years in the locked ward, he absconded when a delivery was being made to the ward and was never heard of again. The commonly held view was that he went to a different part of the country where he reverted back to his previous behaviour.

JOHN

A particularly sad case was the youngest patient on the ward. He was 23 and had been admitted when he was 17. John had been arrested by the police on suspicion of taking women's underwear from clothes lines. On the day he was arrested, he had a pair of women's knickers in his pocket. John protested his innocence saying he had found the knickers. He had a low IQ and was unable to give any coherent explanation as to why, when he saw the knickers in the street, he picked them up. In the area where this occurred there had been a spate of thefts of women's underwear from clothes lines. The reason the police had stopped to question John is because they thought he looked "odd"

Having been assessed, it was felt in view of his low IQ he should be sent to the local mental hospital as he was not competent to stand trial. In all of my conversations with him, he did not display any signs of mental illness. He was of a pleasant disposition and used to ask me about my social life. "Where did you go last night?" "What did you do?"

Endless questions because he was bored. He used to ask how long he was going to stay at the hospital. Again there was no plan, no sense of assessing what his needs were. It seems incredible that, in the late 1960's, this was the approach even though across the UK there had been paradigm shift in attitudes. As previously stated abortion had been legalised, homosexuality decriminalised, capital punishment was abolished, birching suspended, theatre and literature censorship had been liberalised. *Lady Chatterley's Lover* by D H Laurence had been published. Yet when it came to mental illness, it was still acceptable to incarcerate someone on the flimsiest evidence.

In a conversation I had with one of the nurses, he spoke about the injustice of this. This nurse was a laconic Ulsterman. He pointed out there had been no witnesses, no trial, simply some circumstantial evidence and John was sectioned and that was that. His parents were also of limited intelligence and simply accepted the status quo.

This was also the first time I had really encountered the prejudice and narrow- mindedness of some psychiatric nurses. John, from time to time masturbated and was nicknamed "wanker" by some staff. The fact that he was deriving sexual pleasure in the only way available to him seemed lost on many of the staff who considered him to be a sexual pervert. The absurdity of this encapsulates the downside of mental hospitals. The stereotyping of people and the pathologising of behaviour that far from being abnormal was quite the opposite.

I then decided to do something which led me into conflict with the charge nurse of the other shift.

I spoke with John and asked him if it was true that he had not been stealing underwear from clothes lines and was it correct that all he did was find some knickers in the street. He was adamant that this was the case. One of the many things that by now I had learnt in my training was the innocent nature of some people with low intelligence.

Many lack the guile and deviousness of people who have committed crimes.

As a result, I helped him write a letter to his consultant psychiatrist. His handwriting was surprisingly better than I had expected. It was his sentence construction that was the problem. I therefore dictated the letter for him ensuring that I used language and phraseology that was consistent with his speech and thinking. All these years later I can remember the letter virtually verbatim.

Dear Dr McIntosh,

My name is John ...... and I am one of your patients

I have been in this ward for six years for something I haven't done.

If you allow me ground parole I promise I will come back and will not do anything wrong whilst I am out of the ward.

Yours sincerely,

John

There are two things to mention here. The first is that, in those days, there were very few consultant psychiatrists and they had caseloads running into hundreds of patients. Because of the workload, they were preoccupied with the most difficult or acutely ill patients. Someone as compliant and passive as John may have been seen by his consultant on admission, but from then on he would not have been seen unless there was a problem, which with John was not the case. The second point is that ground parole was the term used when the time came for any patient to be trusted to be allowed to leave the ward for short periods, usually an hour to start with and then increasing over time if there were no problems.

I put the letter, sealed in an envelope, in the consultant's correspondence tray in the charge nurses' office. By coincidence, on the day in question I was working overtime on the other charge nurse's shift.

During the course of the afternoon this charge nurse hastily summoned all the staff together and, in a hushed tone, told us that John had written to his consultant and was holding the letter. He warned us that John could not have possibly constructed a letter like this without help and he suspected one of the more recently admitted patients who had a psychopathic disorder encouraged and helped John compose the letter. I intervened and explained that it was I who had helped John and began to explain why. The upshot of this, before I could even get to the end of my first sentence, was to be rounded on by the charge nurse and his deputy accusing me of encouraging a sex offender. I in turn responded by saying that I thought they had no right to open a letter addressed to John's consultant and that I intended to take advice from one of my tutors in the School of Nursing as to what I should do about it.

This was met with even more hostility and eventually the charge nurse and his deputy retreated to his office.

About an hour later, they emerged and in surly terms informed me that the letter had been resealed and placed in the consultant's correspondence tray.

For the rest of the shift I was ignored and I have to say I felt more than uncomfortable, I felt intimidated.

The next day, back on my own shift working with Thomas, my initiative was a matter for discussion. Thomas was sympathetic and admitted that he had never really given much thought as to whether John was innocent of the offence. He did however counsel me and advised that I should have waited until I was on shift with him and talked it through. The charge nurse on the other shift didn't know me and on seeing the letter out of context had felt suspicious, hence his reaction.

A few days later came the ward round where the consultant visited the ward and dealt with any matters the charge nurse drew to her attention. Before going on to explain John's story I want to digress a little.

The fact that a psychiatrist never reviewed literally hundreds of patients was nothing short of a disgrace and it also contributed to many people languishing in hospitals for years when they didn't need to be there.

So, the moment came when Thomas brought to the attention of Dr McIntosh, John's letter. I was not present during the initial discussion. Student nurses were not considered worthy of attending ward rounds. However, Thomas explained my role and the consultant asked to see me. In those days consultants were revered and a student nurse would normally never have the opportunity to converse with one. I was young and not inhibited; I simply gave my perspective on things and readily acknowledged that without my intervention John would have never written his letter.

John was then invited into the ward round. This again is also worthy of some comment. Ward rounds were a kind of star chamber where there was a semi- circle of chairs with the consultant, her senior registrar and a junior doctor together with the charge nurse, a senior manager and a social worker. The patient was never introduced to those present and if, for example, during an interview refreshments were brought in, the tea or coffee was never offered to the patient. It truly was an intimidating and threatening experience. How anyone could feel able to open up and convey to their psychiatrist anything remotely to do with their illness or how they were feeling was beyond me.

Despite this, John answered all of the questions put to him. He reiterated his innocence and promised that, if given ground parole, he would behave himself. The consultant, without referring to anyone, else agreed that he could have one hour ground parole.

I felt vindicated and, later that morning, John was allowed out of the ward. Thomas went to great lengths to explain to John that he must not leave the hospital grounds and he had to be back in an hour. It's worth pausing to think that, after six years, this was the first time he had been out of the ward unescorted, quite a moment. To my surprise, John was back in twenty minutes and said how much he had enjoyed himself. This daily routine went on for some time and I asked him why did he not take the full hour. John explained that he did not have a watch and was worried that, if he did not return on time, ground parole would be withdrawn. Thomas had a spare watch at home, so brought it in the next day and from that time onwards John used the full hour. After several weeks, the ground parole was further extended and John was eventually transferred to an open ward.

Within a year he was discharged back home to his

parents who lived in a town 15 miles away.

Many years later, whilst I was in this town, I saw John who was working as a refuse collector. He recognised me and gave me a cautious smile whilst at the same time affording an anxious glance to his colleagues. I'm sure that John's reaction was one of concern that I might come across and speak with him and that could have resulted in his fellow workers learning about his time in a mental hospital and the reason why he was there. I decided to walk on by and gave John a brief wave and I nodded to him. He smiled, waved and nodded back. I never saw or heard of him again, but I'm not going to deny that even to this day over 50 years later I feel proud of my role in righting a wrong.

A MAN CALLED CARTER

One of my most difficult encounters was with a patient whose surname was Carter, the same as mine. This man was big and powerful and uncommunicative. He suffered from paranoid schizophrenia and was in a state of constant delusion. He thought he was a chair and always sat in the same position in the ward quite isolated from other patents. His posture was bolt upright and he looked straight ahead, very much positioning himself like a chair. I was warned never to approach him and that, if he was left alone, he would not pose any threat.

At meal times, he came to the hatch in the dining room to collect his meal. After he had eaten he would return to his chair. He also was compliant with his medication and, when called to the medicine trolley, he again presented without a problem.

There was an incident that gave me real cause for concern. One day when we were administering the medicines/drugs, I was assisting the staff nurse. When it came to this man's turn, he accepted the medicine from the staff nurse and then, without warning, threw the drugs and the liquid chlorpromazine in my face. He then snarled and said some things that were incomprehensible. I was taken aback and had reeled from the incident, which immediately attracted the attention of the other staff who quickly rallied around me and created a barrier between the patient and myself. One of the experienced nurses spoke with him and asked him to go to his seat. He did this in a quiet but firm manner with which the patient readily complied. The staff then asked me if I had any idea what had provoked this. I replied none at all. I had not had any contact with him and had kept my distance along with the other staff. We then resumed the drug round and afterwards one of the other staff nurses said he had worked out the problem. In those days, people rarely used first names. We referred to each other by our surnames. Me being Carter, the same as this patient, I would often be called to do things "Hey Carter can you give me a hand with the medicine round" or whatever. The use of my surname would have been very common as it was student nurses who always did the "running": "Carter, go to the pharmacy"; "Carter, time to open up the bathrooms" etc. The patient would hear his name being called and then, in turn, would see me responding. This, it was thought aroused his paranoia and he assumed that I was somehow interfering with his life. From then on, Thomas instructed that I was always to be referred to as Peter. There were a number of lessons I learnt from this. The first is that paranoid people can be very dangerous. I had been taught this in the lectures on paranoia but this was a first- hand experience not to be forgotten. The second was the reaction of my colleagues who were quick to rally to my protection and the final one was the manner in which the staff nurse who in a firm but quiet manner had asked the patient to return to his seat. The learning from this is reinforced to me that you can confront issues without being confrontational. It's called de-escalation. Nevertheless it was a chastening experience and one not to be forgotten. Throughout the rest of my time on the ward, there were no further incidents although I kept a weather eye on my namesake's whereabouts.

There was one other incident concerning this man that I should mention. Occasionally we would take some of the patients who were compliant out of the ward on a walk, escorted by several staff. The patients walked in a long line through the hospital grounds, which were extensive. This hospital comprised 200 acres. Along the periphery of the hospital was a stream. One of the nurses suffered from epilepsy which had been well- controlled for many years. He frequently experienced petit mal epilepsy and rarely had grand mals. Petit mal epilepsy is, as the phrase suggests, a mild form of epilepsy, which often manifests itself with mild, twitching of the face, hardly noticeable as the anti-convulsant drugs are doing their job.

On a day when we were out walking, unnoticed by any of us, this nurse who was at the back of the line of walkers suffered a grand mal seizure and fell into the stream. We would have carried on walking had it not been for my namesake who ran up to another colleague and said in a clear and coherent manner "Come quickly, the big attendant has fallen in the ditch". Yet another eye opener and lesson for me.

Despite this man living a tortured existence and being uncommunicative, at a time of crisis he responded perfectly appropriately. He showed concern for a fellow human being. On returning to the ward, Thomas thanked him, however, there was no response. He just sat there like a chair.

CHAS

Like most members of the public, I was familiar with the term psychopath. I was to learn that this is a phrase that is over-used in mainstream society and most people have never come across a true psychopath or understood that they are very dangerous by nature.

One of the most chilling people I have ever had the misfortune to meet was Chas. an eighteen-year-old who truly was a psychopath. At six foot tall, slim of build and good-looking with a charming manner on first encounter, I could have never imagined what a complex, devious and highly dangerous person he was. This young man had been admitted to an open ward with a long history of violent and manipulative behaviour. His consultant psychiatrist was an elderly woman who probably should have retired many years before and had held the view that Chas was misunderstood. He had been referred via the courts after another one of his violent outbursts in which he had badly assaulted an older man. During his time on the open ward, he created difficulties although none of which was initially attributed to him. This involved setting patients off against each other; inciting violence and inveigling himself with the staff. He would often overhear conversations and then relay them back to other patients. An example springs to mind, when two male nurses were making the beds in one of the open dormitories and were discussing a female nurse to whom one of the men was attracted. During the conversation, one of the nurses mentioned that she had recently fallen out with her boyfriend and therefore there might be an opportunity to ask her out for a date.

A few weeks later, at a social event when the male and female patients were allowed to mix, Chas saw the name badge of the nurse and after introducing himself he said that he thought she should know that she had been the subject of a lewd discussion between two male nurses in the hearing of patients. He went on to explain that he knew she had fallen out with her boyfriend and that he (Chas) owed it to her to warn her about the male nurse whom he named. Unsurprisingly, the young nurse was taken aback and upset. She raised it with her ward sister who in turn spoke with the charge nurse on Chas's ward. Without going into the minutiae, there were discussions with the two male nurses who were very angry at having had their conversation overheard. Chas pleaded his innocence, saying he was looking out for the female nurses' best interests. His consultant psychiatrist was supportive of Chas and believed that he was acting with good intentions. The two male nurses, who of course should have never had their conversation within earshot of a patient, met with the young woman and offered their unreserved apologies. The psychopathic behaviour continued with patients fighting each other and making life difficult for the staff all of which could be attributed to Chas but not in a way that could result in any sanction or with him being admonished by his consultant psychiatrist, as there was no direct evidence. And then one day there was an incident that began to trigger events that led to a dramatic conclusion.

A male nurse was checking the toilet area of the ward. This was a common task as toilet areas were a place of self-harm and of tension where patients could spark off each other. Chas was in the toilet area and was overheard by the nurse inciting another patient to smash the fire alarm in the ward. This would have created a major upheaval with the ward being evacuated and the fire brigade automatically being alerted to attend the hospital. The nurse intervened and asked the patient who was being manipulated to go into the day room. The nurse then informed Chas that his behaviour would be brought to the attention of his consultant. At this Chas exploded with rage and seriously assaulted the nurse raining punches and kicks on him. The nurse was badly injured and it took several other nurses to restrain Chas. Following this he was transferred to the locked ward.

Despite this, the consultant still had a view that this young man was misunderstood and that more effort should be made to relate and help him. Whilst on the locked ward he created further problems all of which were done in a way that he could not be held accountable for. After several weeks on the locked ward, his consultant agreed at the request of Chas to transfer him back to an open ward. The level of his deviousness and his ability to manipulate was as staggering as was the inability of his consultant to see this.

There was a further incident that brought things to a head. When visiting the patient social centre, Chas became involved in an altercation with another patient resulting in Chas picking a heavy water jug and smashing into the face of the patient, inflicting serious injury.

Again, it took a number of male nurses to restrain him and he was taken back to the locked ward. There followed a series of discussions with Thomas the highly experienced charge nurse, the consultant and senior management. Astonishingly, Chas was pleading self-defence and the consultant still not understanding the gravity of the situation. A member of staff drew up a petition and asked staff to sign it. The petition was addressed to the consultant and it expressed no confidence in her ability to grasp the seriousness of the situation and put it to her that if matters continued it was only a matter of time before someone sustained a life-changing injury or, worse, was killed.

In the build up to this there were two more incidents. The first was when Chas had asked to be allowed into the dormitory to retrieve something from his locker and the orderly who was cleaning the floor explained that he would have to wait as he had only just polished the floor and it was not yet dry. Chas flew into a violent rage and punched the heavy oak dormitory door, breaking with his fist one of the solid stantions. This was really chilling as that punch could have easily killed someone.

The second incident was when a patient in a seclusion room was passed some matches and he, in turn, set fire to the mattress potentially putting not only himself at risk as he was locked in but also the other patents and staff. The fire was quickly detected and extinguished by the staff but not before the locked ward was evacuated causing significant mayhem with a number of patients having to be restrained as they were attempting to abscond. The patient who had set fire to his mattress told the staff that it was Chas who had passed the matches to him through the small observation hatch.

As a result of this, the consultant agreed to a second opinion. A consultant psychiatrist from the high secure hospital, Rampton was asked to carry out the assessment.

On doing so, this specialist in psychopathic behaviour reached the view that Chas suffered from a psychopathic disorder so severe that he believed that he would eventually kill someone or commission someone to kill on his behalf. He recommended that Chas be transferred with immediate effect to Rampton. This, of course, was welcomed by the staff on the locked ward and throughout the hospital. The consultant, who had been so unable to accept she had been duped by Chas, had no option but to agree and that very day a van arrived from Rampton with two male nurses and a driver to take Chas away. Chas had been unaware that this was going to happen, and had been in a relaxed frame of mind following the interview he had with the psychiatrist, believing that once again he had managed to convince a psychiatrist that he had been misunderstood. For fear of a backlash, Chas was not informed of the decision to transfer him to Rampton. At about 3pm, the two nurses from Rampton arrived at the ward. They had a meeting with Thomas at which some of us were allowed to be present. Thomas outlined the issues, although the two nurses had already been briefed by their consultant psychiatrist.

They then entered the day room, and Thomas led them to Chas. Thomas explained to Chas that he was being transferred to another hospital and that these two nurses were going to escort him. Chas looked confused and eyed the two male nurses. I should mention at this stage that, in those days, nurses in high secure hospitals wore uniforms akin to prison officers and were very experienced at working with highly disturbed and violent patients. Chas looked quite chastened as the two nurses told him to come with them. There was no physical contact and Thomas had arranged for the few possessions Chas had to be bagged up whilst the paper work was being completed. Chas asked if he could see his consultant (presumably as he was hoping for another throw of the dice imploring her to allow him to stay). Thomas said, "Chas we've passed that point. You are on your way". He then walked out of the ward into the back of the van which was in the secure court yard and proceeded to Rampton.

I was intrigued by the sequence of events. First, the consultant from Rampton who had assessed Chas was so concerned that he had arranged an admission straight away; hence the arrival of the Rampton staff by mid-afternoon. I was also intrigued by the reaction of Chas. No violence or protest. Was it that he realised that there was no way the decision could be overturned? Was it that he had worked out that any show of violence could only make matters worse for him? As the van pulled away from the hospital, I felt in a strange way a sense of sadness. Not that I had any sympathy for him but more for the tragedy of the situation. What was it that would make someone go through life constantly causing disharmony and conflict? What had happened to him in early childhood that had resulted in him becoming such a devious and manipulative person? I also wondered what was going through his mind on the way up to Rampton. He must have worked out that he was going to a place more akin to a prison than a hospital and on arriving he must have quickly realised that he was going to be there for a very long time because that was the lot of most of the other patients.

Many years later, a member of staff who knew Chas from his time at our hospital was visiting Rampton and, in one of the units, he spotted Chas who also recognised him. On seeing the nurse, Chas stood up to say hello and was immediately reproached by a nurse ordering him to sit down. The feedback we received was that Chas was a shadow of his former self. The arrogance had gone and in many respects he was a cowed person. I'm not for one moment saying I approve of this. However, I am sure that, had it not been for the petition from the staff, it was only a matter of time before there would have been an even more severe catastrophe over and above those I have already described. I assume Chas remained in the hospital for many years and would have only been released when deemed no longer to be a threat.

As for the consultant, her credibility and authority was shot to pieces and not long afterwards she retired.

SYDNEY

Although there are countless other anecdotes I could give there is one more that I wish to mention. There are many words and phrases that are easily bandied about and are in such frequent use that they actually diminish the true meaning of the word or phrase. For example, the use of the term OCD, obsessive compulsive disorder. This is a crippling disease, but people use the term to describe the behaviour of people who like things to be neat and tidy. Recently a number of celebrities have been using the term. The footballer David Beckham once described himself as suffering from OCD. He does not. OCD is a terrifying condition and it can render some people incapable of living any semblance of a normal life. Sydney was such a man who was tormented by his condition. To get into bed at night took him hours. The rituals he followed involved trying to ensure his sheets and pillows did not have any creases. His hand-washing equally took hours along with many other rituals.

Despite every effort of the staff to try to work with him, all proved unsuccessful. He was therefore left to his own devices and his whole life was one of rituals and repetition and torment. Like many others, I attempted to speak with him to see if I could get through but to no avail. I make reference to this at the stage because at the time of writing, whilst there has been a healthy raising of awareness by high profile people of the need to recognise mental health issues and to try to rid society of the stigma associated with it. the downside is the number of people are using terms inappropriately and there is a current trend to pathologise normal behaviour. This is as unhelpful as is the stigma associated with mental health. We need to de-stigmitise but let's not turn mental health into a fashion accessory.

And so my time on this ward came to an end and my training continued. Different wards, different experiences, I loved it all.

Chapter 4: The Incident

As I have attempted to reflect, most of my experiences were positive and the modern-day portrayal of mental hospitals as being uniformly uncaring and punitive institutions is simply not accurate. Sure they were overcrowded, understaffed and some of the practices were institutional. Most of those practices were as a result of a failure of policy-makers to move with the times. Nurses and other staff were trained in a model of containment, as there was very little in the way of alternatives. However, as the development of more sophisticated drugs emerged with a more enlightened approach in the care of people with mental health problems, the people who were also left behind were the staff. There was little or no updated training and no investment in new ways of working. I'm not sure what those in authority expected. Were the staff going to change the way they had been trained by a process of osmosis? In any other walk of life, when new techniques and methods evolve, firms, companies and organisations embark on a change management programme with the staff. This did not happen with staff working in mental hospitals, hence a failure to modernise and move on.

There was an incident that personified the insular nature of mental hospitals that crystallises why they were subject to so much criticism and derision.

At the hospital I trained at, there was a longstanding relationship with Bart's hospital in London. During the Second World War, Bart's was evacuated to the Hill End hospital St Albans, which was in the country because Bart's, being in the heart of London, was vulnerable to air raids. After the war, they returned to their site in London but the link was maintained and, every three months, six student nurses from Bart's were seconded to the hospital to do a three-month placement as part of their nurse training.

Back in those days, Bart's nurses were predominantly from well-heeled families. Many had private education and came from professional families. It was interesting to observe the contrast in cultures of the quite sophisticated young women coalescing with people who came from predominantly working-class backgrounds. In my experience, most of the Bart's nurses were people that had very good values and skills, judging people on how they behaved as opposed to their background. These young women, in most cases, were highly ethical and personified everything that is to be admired in nursing. Many of them because, of their background and education, could have chosen many other career paths but nursing was their ambition and love.

I will now go into the incident that I have already referred to. A nineteen-year-old Bart's nurse who was three weeks into her secondment was asked to go to another ward to borrow a piece of equipment.

On entering the ward via the dormitory entrance, she was making her way through to the day room when she heard the sound of a woman in a distressed manner coming from the bathroom area. She went to investigate and to her horror found a male nurse sexually assaulting an 88-year-old woman. The male nurse had his fingers in her vagina and was making some lewd comments and the elderly woman was in a state of abject distress. The nurse pleaded with the man to stop and he in turn was taken aback at being discovered. The Bart's nurse fled from the ward in a state of shock and distress and, on returning to her ward, reported the matter to her ward sister who in turn immediately called the deputy matron. As a result, the male nurse was summoned to the matron's office whereupon he totally denied the incident.

It was decided that he should be suspended whilst an investigation was carried out. This resulted in uproar from many of the staff of the hospital. The accused nurse made a counter-allegation that the Bart's nurse was a troublemaker and all that he had been doing in the bathroom was assisting the elderly patient who was upset over something and he was reassuring her.

The combined Trade Unions COHSE, NUPE and NALGO

insisted that the male nurse be reinstated and that the Bart's nurse should be suspended for making such an outrageous allegation against a colleague who had an unblemished record. The Bart's nurse was immediately despatched back to London. She was adamant that the incident she had so graphically described was true and she had no intention of withdrawing her allegation.

A union meeting was called in the main hall of the hospital which over 300 people attended. The atmosphere was febrile with people threatening strike action. This coincided with a number of inquiries into other mental hospitals following the exposure of horrendous atrocities. The reader may look at the investigations into hospitals such as Ely in Cardiff and St Augustine's in Canterbury. It was as a result of these national inquires that the staff were so incensed with the view that nurses in particular were vulnerable to unsubstantiated allegations and if this man was not reinstated then we would all be vulnerable and basically where would it all end.

Now you need to bear in mind that I was a student, 19 years old and already had been seen suspect by some staff because of my actions in relation to John the young man who had been detained in the hospital on spurious grounds. I plucked up the courage in the meeting to give an alternative view on matters. I put it to the meeting that surely the management had a duty to investigate the allegation if only to clear the nurse of the allegations. This was met with derision from some of those present with comments such as "whose side are you on?" In addition, there were asides about my political affiliations. The Vietnam War was raging and I had been on some anti-war demonstrations in London. In addition, I had long hair and did not fit the stereotype that some of the traditional and middle-aged nurses assumed nurses should have. Comments such as "We don't want to listen to a longhaired communist" were made. On reflection, it was all really absurd but I persevered. I put it to the meeting that we should look at the facts. Did we really believe that a student nurse who had no previous contact with the male nurse who she was accusing would concoct such a terrible allegation if there was no truth in it? We were asked to believe that this student nurse has made up the most serious allegation against someone she had never met before and, when subjected to the most horrendous pressure, had stuck with her account. Why would she do this, what was the motive? In my view it didn't make sense.

Despite my intervention, which was disregarded, the meeting overwhelmingly passed a vote demanding that the male nurse should be reinstated.

This, in turn, was put to the management, who incidentally were feeling under some significant pressure as the local newspaper had been informed of the allegation and it was front-page news. It also says something about the closed nature of institutions that the police were not called in. The management succumbed to the demands of the staff and the nurse was reinstated and the matter was considered closed.

This, in my view, was truly shocking. The whole incident was the subject of on-going discussion among the staff. Some people felt the Bart's nurse had genuinely misunderstood what she had witnessed in the bathroom; others felt that she was nothing other than a middle-class trouble-maker who got what she deserved being sent back to Bart's with her reputation in tatters.

Then one evening in the hospital social club, a charge nurse of longstanding experience and near retirement was listening in on yet another discussion about the incident. He casually said, "I believe the Bart's nurse". This took most people aback. When asked why, he referred to me, quoting what I had said: "Are we really to believe that this student nurse from Bart's would make such a devastating allegation against someone she has never met before?" Like me, "Jock" the charge nurse believed the student nurse. Needless to say, this pleased me and it also set those present thinking. Here was a well-respected charge nurse saying the unthinkable according to most members of staff. This was another learning experience for me that was to stand me in good stead later in my career. It demonstrates how a group of staff can get carried away with a sense of injustice and, if no one from senior management is prepared to give an alternative view, the momentum is with the caucus, irrespective of the need for proper process.

Within a year the male nurse left the hospital. There is however a sequel to the issue.

Fifteen years later, this man was again the subject of an identical allegation at another hospital, only this time the Director of Nursing Service had more professionalism and integrity about him than the managers that had so easily given in to the demands of the staff. Due to the seriousness of the allegation, the police were called and, following an extensive investigation, the man was charged with sexual assault of an elderly woman (patient) and the matter proceeded to court. The result was that the jury found him guilty and he was given a substantial prison sentence. I have occasionally reflected on the student nurse from Bart's who made the allegation and my wish/hope is that someone made the connection and informed her. In reality, the chances were very slim but you never know!

Chapter 5: The Chinese takeaway.

As my training progressed and I grew in confidence, I was part of a group of staff that were trying new ways of working: more personalised choice for patients, more trips out of the hospital. We began to take patients to the local swimming pool and occasionally the local pub.

During the summer months it had become fashionable for wards to have a party. This usually consisted of a BBQ and patients from other wards were invited, as were relatives and friends. I was working on a long-stay ward and, in conversation with a colleague, he asked me how was my weekend. Among other things I mentioned that I had a Chinese takeaway on the Saturday night.

This prompted a patient, Aubrey, who overheard the conversation to enquire as to what was a Chinese takeaway. I explained it to him and he was intrigued. He went on to explain that his father had been in the colonial service and had been in Singapore from 1890 where Aubrey was born in 1895 where he had spent a lot of his childhood until being sent to boarding school in England. Aubrey had been in the hospital for many years. He suffered from manic depressive psychosis (now called bipolar disorder) and had at times been very disturbed. Although his illness in its severest form had burnt out, he was still subject to deep depression when he would be in a state of almost total withdrawal. His manic phases, however, had long ceased. He was, as were so many other patients, institutionalised after decades of being hospitalised. Aubrey went on to explain that he loved Chinese food although he had not had any since he was a teenager and would welcome the opportunity to try some. This got me thinking. Instead of the usual BBQ why not have a Chinese takeaway brought to the ward. There was always a budget because, in addition to the food that was provided by the hospital catering department, crates of beer were purchased along with delicacies that were not available from the hospital kitchen. I ran the idea past the charge nurse, Pat, who yet again was a congenial Irishman. He was highly amused and queried whether the patients would eat it. I felt sure they would. He then wondered would the Chinese takeaway be prepared to deliver it to the hospital. I said we could start by asking them.

I then spoke to the patients. Most were indifferent but some said they would be prepared to try it.

That evening, I went down to the takeaway and asked the proprietor if he could deliver food for 60 people to the local mental hospital. Now this is the thing about Chinese people that I have always liked and admired. He didn't hesitate to say yes. There was no incredulity, no hesitation. He simply said, "You order, I deliver". I explained that I would get back to him. The next day I spoke with Pat, and we agreed that, whilst we would go ahead with the order, we should also order some of the usual food from the hospital catering department, in case the patients and some of their visitors didn't like the Chinese option. When the catering manager saw the order for the food, he called the ward to say that we had not ordered enough. It was a 30-bedded ward and with some other patients and visitors we needed to cater for 60. The charge nurse explained that we were trying something different and informed him of the Chinese takeaway. This was met with a hostile reaction along the lines of "What do you think you are doing; this should not be allowed". Apparently, he went on and on and said he was going to bring it to the attention of 'higher management'.

The charge nurse relayed the story to me and said in a very worried manner that he thought we were in for trouble. How right he was. The catering manager, in addition to complaining to the deputy chief male nurse, also brought it to the attention of the branch secretaries of NUPE and COHSE. These were the two unions that most hospital staff were members of.

The issues were as follows. The Unions said this is the thin edge of the wedge and what would happen if all the wards started to order takeaway food. In addition, what about food hygiene regulations, how did we know that the patients were not going to get food poisoning? All of this, of course, was absolute nonsense but demonstrated the resistance to change and how truly pathetic arguments could be used in order to prevent change. Therefore, the deputy chief male nurse called a meeting and Pat the charge nurse was asked to attend. By now he was even more anxious. He was part of a generation that did not rock the boat. He was a good nurse, very kind to the patients, and was clearly disconcerted by what was happening. Although I was young, I began to feel for him and I put to him that if this was going to create difficulties perhaps we should drop the idea. Just as we were about to discuss the pros and cons, the office phone rang and he had to take a call about an impending transfer of one of our patients who was elderly and unwell to a geriatric ward which was more equipped to nurse him.

After the phone call, Pat said that he had a change of mind and that he couldn't see why the original plan shouldn't stand. He asked me if I wanted to attend the meeting, which of course I did.

Present at the meeting were the catering manager, the branch secretary of NUPE, the deputy chief male nurse and a man who was a charge nurse but was also acting in the capacity of assistant chief male nurse, covering annual leave. I knew this man disliked me. The attitude was hostile and sneering, particularly towards me. Pat the charge nurse was brilliant. He set out how the idea had emerged and said that he felt we should give it a go. The Union official spoke about the erosion of jobs, which Pat quickly dealt with saying it was ridiculous. The person who was most hostile was the assistant chief male nurse who used all manner of arguments to shoot the idea down. Some of the things he said were so bizarre that they were laughable. He thought that Chinese food could have detrimental effect on the mental health of the patients. He also spoke about the danger of food poisoning and had a disparaging view of Chinese food that he kept referring to as "chinky muck".

I pointed out that the restaurant was subject to food hygiene regulations and was always very busy and there were no problems, so it was illogical to suggest that the patients would be susceptible to food poisoning. As for the detrimental effect on their mental state, I put to him how could some rice noodles and prawn crackers upset someone's mental state. During the meeting, I had to endure a number of snide remarks about me personally. "You supported that Bart's nurse with her false allegations". "You helped that patient write a letter to his consultant" and so on. Throughout Pat was a star. We were however not getting anywhere, and it looked like we were going to be overruled when the assistant chief male nurse asked us if we had sought the permission of

Dr Stephenson, the consultant psychiatrist for the ward. We said that it had not occurred to us that this would be necessary. It was at this point that something landed in our lap. The assistant chief male nurse said that he intended to ask Dr Stephenson for his opinion on this. Dr Stephenson' office was on the same corridor and by sheer fluke of timing, when our chief prosecutor opened the office door to see if Dr Stephenson was available he happened to be walking by. He was invited into the meeting. Before describing what happened some background information on the consultant is important.

He was elderly and walked on two sticks. In his younger days, he had played rugby for Ireland and for many years held a number of rugby world records such as the player who had kicked the most points and the most consecutive appearances. Due to his prolonged rugby career, his injuries, as he aged, had left him with several arthritic problems, hence his poor mobility. I had already met him and we had a number of conversations about his rugby career. It was sad to see this man, who in his day had been a tremendous athlete and was one of the world's most feared rugby players to be so infirmed.

After taking his seat in the meeting, the assistant chief male nurse explained along the following lines.

"Carter has this idea that, instead of a ward BBQ, he

should arrange for a Chinese takeaway to deliver food to the ward, and I've only just discovered that he has not asked your permission". "Run that past me again" said Dr Stephenson who looked slightly incredulous. When it was explained, his response was "What a wonderful idea Carter". Nelson, the assistant chief male nurse was seriously taken aback by this reaction and then went on to ask Dr Stephenson if he did not fear that it could have a detrimental effect on the patients' mental state. "Good God man, how ridiculous" was the reply. Dr Stephenson then turned to me and asked if he would be invited. I blagged it and said that we intended to invite him but, as there was still some resistance from those in authority, we were not sure if it was going to go ahead.

"Well, I sincerely hope it does go ahead," said Dr Stephenson. It was at this point the deputy chief male nurse intervened and said that he thought it should go ahead.

We were thrilled. Dr Stephenson said he was looking forward to it and asked if he could throw in a crate of beer to which we said it would be gratefully received!

On walking back to the ward, I asked Pat what had happened to make him change his mind as, when we were in the office just prior to the phone call, he appeared to be on the verge of calling it all off.

He agreed this was the case but it was during the phone call that he reflected on the absurdity of the situation and had decided that he would support my initiative.

We were then full steam ahead. I went back to the Chinese takeaway and negotiated a good deal.

As the day approached, I began to have doubts. What if the patients didn't like it? What if there was an outbreak of food poisoning? These doubts were with me right up until the moment the food arrived. The restaurateur provided copious amounts of food and, much to my relief, the patients, their visitors and the staff scoffed the lot. They loved it.

And so ended the Chinese takeaway saga. There was no food poisoning and unsurprisingly it did not herald a mass movement away from hospital food to a takeaway mentality! The whole episode personifies just how difficult change could be in the old mental hospitals. The powers that be had a vested interest in keeping things closed and anyone seeking to change or influence the culture would have to push against real intimidation and personal vilification.

Chapter 6: Patient outings, activities and holidays.

As with all mental hospitals, there was a department that was responsible for arranging outings, activities and holidays for the patients.

These were a mixture of coach trips to the coast or to visit places of historical interest such as Blenheim Palace and exchange stays with other mental hospitals where patients would have two weeks in another hospital.

The proprietors of the venues for the day trips were always very welcoming. I suspect this was mainly due to the enthusiasm of the woman who organised everything.

She was a registered nurse, Sister Brewster. This woman was a delight. A model of professionalism and enthusiasm. Her many years of experience meant that the places she chose were always suitable and she had developed a good relationship with staff at all of the venues and locations.

Nurses volunteered to go on these trips. Student nurses were encouraged to do so. It meant a day out of the hospital and, if it was on your day off, you were paid overtime.

One of the most sought-after trips was the annual outing

to the Epsom Derby. This famous horse race attracted tens of thousands of people and, in addition to the horse racing, there was a large fun fair and a whole array of bars, stalls and food outlets. We travelled with a packed lunch that was prepared by the hospital catering department and was always substantial. The trip down to Epsom was uneventful with Sister Brewster instructing the patients and the staff on where we should gather for lunch and, importantly, what time we needed to be back on the coach at the end of the day. Each patient had spending money that was either from their earnings from the "factories" or from their savings.

As soon as we arrived at the racecourse, the patients simply disappeared into the crowd. I expressed my concern to Sister Brewster who instantly reassured me, "Don't worry dear the patients will all return at 12.30 for their lunch and I'm not expecting to lose any during the course of the day". She went on to say that people constantly underestimate those who have longstanding mental health problems and the more responsibility you gave to these people the more they will take responsibility for their own behaviour. Sister Brewster knew her stuff and at 12.30 all of the patients (and staff) returned to the coach for lunch. It was a gloriously sunny May day. I spent time wandering around between watching some of the racing and touring the fun fair. One of the booths was a striptease show and, to my amazement, a number of patients were queuing up to go and see the show. One of the patients who I knew really well was in the queue and I spoke with him. It transpired that six of the patients had been into the show continuously since it opened just before lunch. It had never occurred to me that these men would have any interest in sex. The spartan world of mental hospitals and the lack of any significant contact between men and women meant that the subject or concept of these people having any interest in the opposite sex was never discussed.

It all seemed pretty harmless to me and the cashier on the booth was highly amused that these six kept on seeing the same show that was repeated every half hour. I was minded to go and see if I could negotiate a discount but thought better of it.

The day was highly enjoyable and everyone found his or her way back to the coach in good time. Sr Brewster's attention to detail was really impressive. Many of the patients were on high doses of chlorpromazine (Largactil) and one of the effects of this drug is that it renders the skin of people vulnerable to sun burn. Being a hot day, Sr Brewster had given all of the patients a heavy coating of Uvistat, a powerful sun block. A small detail, but one that says everything about her caring approach. It was some time later that I saw the effects of Largactil on a patient who had been in the gardens on a hot day without any protection; the sunburn was horrendous.

As we were coming to the end of our journey, Sr Brewster came and sat with me. She wanted to hear my observations of the day. She was not only keen to know if I had enjoyed it but did I have any suggestions as to how we could make it better. Were there any lessons to be learnt, was there anything I felt we shouldn't have done? This was yet another valuable lesson in my development. Sr Brewster had explained that students saw things with fresh eyes and their feedback was invaluable. It also said something about her values in recognising that every member of the team had something to offer. As it was, there was nothing I could add and neither was there anything that I thought we shouldn't have been doing.

I have mentioned the swopping between hospitals to give patients a holiday. This on first hearing I thought was truly bizarre. Why could anyone think that going off to another hospital for two weeks was a good idea? How wrong was I.

I was approached by a senior nurse manager who asked me if I would like to be part of the three-man team that was going to be on the exchange visit to Pen Y Fal hospital in Abergavenny. I jumped at the chance. The form was that we set off in a coach with 40 long-stay patients and half way to Abergavenny we rendezvoused with a coach full of patients from South Wales and we swopped over. On arriving at the hospital we were billeted in the ward that had been vacated. The patients immediately settled in. Each day apart from the weekends we went on an excursion. We visited places all over South Wales: Tintern Abbey, the Gower peninsular, Barry Island and so on. The patients loved it. We also made copious visits to country pubs.

There was, however, one major hiccup with what was otherwise a good holiday. On arrival, one of our patients went missing. Despite an extensive search of the hospital grounds, he could not be found. The police were notified and they too drew a blank. The very elderly and highly experienced charge nurse, Jim said that he thought the patient would be making his way back to our hospital and sure enough nearly two weeks later this is what happened. On arrival in Abergavenny he had instantly decided he didn't like it, so started to walk back. This was 100 miles away and he tramped through the day and slept rough often in telephone boxes. He scrounged food and drink along the way and arrived back in an unkempt state but otherwise was fine. This again was something that intrigued me. Never in my wildest imagination would I have thought this man in his late 60's and having been in hospital for over thirty years would have had the wherewithal to find his way back to our hospital.

It was a fascinating experience. One of the things I most remember was taking three of the patients to the top of the Sugar Loaf, a mountain near Abergavenny in the Brecon Beacons. It was a long hike with a climb of 580 metres and, despite the lack of physical fitness of my three companions, it was quite an adventure that they thoroughly enjoyed. The other thing that I had not expected is that we were paid an additional two weeks wages. The view of the management was that we were away from home for two weeks and not really off duty so this was the appropriate way of recompensing us.

The following year on the same exchange visit there was a tragedy when a patient suffering from paranoid schizophrenia who had been quiet and compliant for years un-expectedly attempted suicide whilst at Pen Y Val. He slit his throat and wrists and cut his penis off. The loss of blood was immense. Despite this, he lived and was eventually transferred back to our hospital where he remained in the locked ward for many years as a result of his suicide attempt. The young student nurse who found him was severely traumatised although with good support came through it. Thus the nature of severe and enduring mental illness was brought into sharp relief. The underlying paranoid delusions, the hallucinations had triggered something that could not have been foreseen or predicted and thus not prevented.

Chapter 7: Treatments and therapies

DRUGS

The primary treatment for mental illness of a psychotic nature was neuroleptic drugs, otherwise known as anti-psychotics. Chlorpromazine was discovered in 1950 and was the first anti-psychotic drug. Its introduction is widely heralded as one of the great advances in the history of psychiatry. Chlorpromazine changed the whole approach to the treatment of psychosis across the world. By ameliorating the symptoms of conditions such as schizophrenia, it opened up the ability to have a non-custodial approach to the treatment and care of people with severe and enduring mental health problems.

The discovery of chlorpromazine is interesting and is often described as serendipitous. A French surgeon Henri Laborit was experimenting with several compounds as a pre anaesthetic agent prior to surgery one of which was chlorpromazine. Laborit observed that chlorpromazine induced calmness to patients. As a result two psychiatrists working at St Anne's Hospital in Paris, Jean Dealy and Pierre Deniker began to use the drug in the treatment of people suffering from Schizophrenia and mania. The results were revolutionary and in a series of reports that first appeared in 1952 heralded in a worldwide change in the treatment of these conditions.

In addition to chlorpromazine, a whole new generation of drugs was beginning to emerge in the 1960's. The pharmaceutical industry was investing more in research and anti-depressants such as amitriptyline and drugs to help with anxiety such as chlordiazepoxide (Librium) were making huge inroads into conditions that hitherto had poor access to treatments.

Of particular significance was the development of depot injections. These were drugs that were for the treatment of people suffering from psychotic illnesses such as schizophrenia. The drug was contained in a thick oily substance that was injected deep into the gluteal muscle of the buttock. The medication was then slowly absorbed into the blood stream over the course of several weeks. This was a huge step forward as it obviated the need for patients who required these drugs to have to take them several times a day. In addition, patients who were reluctant to take anti-psychotic medication and who would only do so after considerable encouragement or, in rare cases, it was forcibly administered could now not have to face the daily trauma of administration against their will.

Without these drugs, the more enlightened approach to

psychiatry would have simply not happened. By managing the symptoms of illnesses such as schizophrenia, particularly by ameliorating the delusions and hallucinations associated with it the behaviour was significantly modified thus enabling doctors and nurses to be able to help people live a more normal life.

Had it not been for these drugs the closure programme of mental hospitals would not have emerged.

This is important to recognise, as the "anti-psychiatry" movement from the late 60's onwards frequently stereotyped psychiatrists as nothing more than doping agents that lacked humanity. This is a case of selectively pulling out the worst practices of psychiatric care and lumping everyone together. I met some inspirational psychiatrists who were at the forefront of the modernisation of mental health care and were leading exponents of community-based psychiatry helping people to thrive and enjoy productive lives without necessarily needing in patient care. The demonization of psychiatrists specifically and mental health care more generally did a huge disservice to countless hardworking, skilful and conscientious people.

There were down-sides to the drugs. There are examples of patients being prescribed excessive doses of these drugs that rendered patients not only compliant but also incapable of doing even the most basic tasks of daily living. The "chemical cosh" as it was commonly known did much to prejudice the public and policy makers against the use of these drugs. It was not the drugs that were the problem. It was poor prescribing by the few who could not see that a new era had dawned. In addition, many of these drugs had distressing side effects (extrapyramidal reactions): the most common were Parkinson-like symptoms, tardive dyskinesia, drowsiness, obesity, to mention but a few. This necessitated patients having to take other drugs to counter the side effects. By way of example, benztropine (Cogentin) was used to counter the parkinsonian-like symptoms.

I could dilate at length on the use of drugs but this is not the purpose of this book. The Internet can provide the reader with all of the information needed. My only comment, in addition to those I have already made, is that people with severe and enduring mental illness have a life span 10 to 20 years less than people who do not and that anti-psychotic medication is a significant contributor to this phenomenon. This is something that would be unacceptable in the treatment of other conditions and says much about the taxonomy order of those with mental illness. Whilst there are side effects of many of the drugs used in other branches of medicine, I would suggest that it would be unacceptable for there to be such significant difficulties with many other drugs. I believe it is because of the lower order of priority in relation to mental illness, drugs are being authorised with these significant side effects that in other specialities might not be unacceptable.

More research needs to be undertaken to develop drugs that treat the mental illness but do not have these distressing and debilitating side effect. To do this requires significant financial investment, which currently does not appear to be forthcoming.

ELECTRO-CONVULSIVE THERAPY (ECT)

ECT is a term that is widely known by the public but rarely understood.

The use of ECT has dropped dramatically over the past 50 years and many psychiatrists have either never prescribed ECT or have not done so for many years. It was used predominantly for the treatment of intractable depression or for mania and, in some cases, hard-to-treat schizophrenia.

I will state at the outset that I am not a fan of ECT. I believe that the approach should be to understand why a person is depressed and then seek to resolve the issue.

There is, however, a lot of mythology about ECT.

Hollywood films over the years depict patients fighting against being given ECT with the patient being strapped to a table, a gag tied to their mouth and an electric shock administered over the temporal lobe of the brain causing the patient to have a severe fit. The fit depicted is usually violent with nurses holding the patient down. The reality is very different.

Patients are given an anaesthetic and are asleep when the electrodes are placed on the temples and the shock is administered. The patient is also given a muscle relaxant and the "fit" is, in fact, a series of twitches that usually last between ten to thirty seconds. The patient is constantly under the supervision of an anaesthetist and an experienced psychiatric nurse as well as the psychiatrist who administers the shock.

Prior to ECT, the patient undergoes a thorough physical examination to ensure they can be anaesthetised. The shock is, in fact, the least of the worries.

The interesting thing is that I have met so many patients who actually ask for ECT. I have seen people who suffer from recurring depression literally beg their psychiatrist for ECT so as to lift their depression. The fact is that in many cases it does and the benefits can last for several years. Then when the black dog of depression (as poignantly described by Winston Churchill) sets in, the request for ECT is made. It is often used with older people who are depressed, with good outcomes.

All of this is quite at odds with the perception of the public who, as I have said, have had their understanding of ECT influenced by movies. Furthermore, psychiatrists are divided over its effectiveness and the associated ethics of using an approach which is the subject to widespread controversy. In some countries the use is highly regulated resulting in a very low use such as the Netherlands and Italy. Some countries such as Slovenia do not use it at all.

INSULIN THERAPY

This therapy is now no longer in use. Up until the late 1960's it was, however, used extensively by one of the psychiatrists at the hospital that I trained at. It involved injecting a patient with insulin to introduce a diabetic coma. It was used for patients suffering from schizophrenia or depression by this psychiatrist. It was in fact a very dangerous intervention and needed highly experienced psychiatric nurses to administer it. A failure to monitor the coma could have had disastrous consequences. In those days there were no national guidelines or protocols, hence there were wide variations in approach. Some psychiatrists used insulin therapy over many weeks whilst other used it as a one-off. Either way it was ineffective, but the placebo effect for a small minority of patients who thought they were receiving evidence-based treatment undoubtedly helped lift their mood.

LEUCOTOMY

By the time I commenced my training leucotomies were a thing of the past. This was a surgical intervention that involved cutting some of the nerve fibres at the front of the brain with the intention of treating intractable mental illness. The impact on the illness was virtually nil. However, patients were rendered compliant which at the time was considered to be a good outcome as opposed to a patient remaining in a disturbed state. The human debris from a failed intervention was tragic to witness. No matter how well-intended, once it was realised how catastrophic this intervention was, it should have been stopped years before. This did not happen and worldwide thousands of people had severe brain damage as a result of their leucotomy. I nursed many patients in this state. Truly heart-rending.

ART AND OCCUPATIONAL THERAPY

I was very fortunate that at my hospital there was a thriving art and occupational therapy department. These were an oasis of creativity. The patients thrived and derived much pleasure and help. I have always enjoyed working with art therapists and OT's.

By nature, they are creative and tolerant people who tend to see the positive in most situations. As part of my placement I too joined in the creative therapies and made a four-legged stool, which I proudly gave to my mother. These were fun places but there were not enough of them and very few patients were able to avail themselves of the undoubted benefit these therapies provided.

I worked with many patients who were acutely ill and derived huge benefit from music therapy, painting and woodwork. These therapies were particularly helpful for people who suffered from the neurosis group of illnesses and conditions. For the reader who is not familiar with the groupings and categorisation of mental illness, the difference between psychosis and neurosis is insight. People suffering from schizophrenia and bi-polar disorder often lack insight into their conditions, particularly during periods when they are acutely unwell. Whereas people suffering from anxiety state, eating disorders or depression have insight and awareness.

Many patients who were depressed may not have touched a paintbrush or a musical instrument since their school days and it always fascinated me how these interventions helped their mental state. There is still a huge underinvestment in this type of therapy.

INDUSTRIAL THERAPY

I have already referred to this: the fact that it brought income into hospitals was a significant driver in their development. Most patients really enjoyed their daily visits to the "factories" and would often be seen queuing up each morning ready for work. Patients were paid to work although I doubt if there was an even sharing of the profits. Nevertheless, the work was important. It got patients out of the wards: self-esteem was raised and many patients, who for years had been institutionalised, began to realise long-lost potential. At the hospital I trained at there was an employment relations officer who went out to employers and in time a significant number of patients were employed full-time outside in general society. Eventually some were discharged although it was interesting that some patients who functioned to a high degree outside the hospital were so institutionalised that they had no wish to live independently.

PSYCHOLOGY AND PSYCHOTHERAPY

From the mid 60's, the growth of psychology services was gathering pace. In most hospitals there was very little investment but year on year it increased. This in turn led increasingly to the introduction of psychotherapy to mental hospitals. In my experience it's unfortunate that both psychologists and psychotherapists struggled to make an impact in mental hospitals. They were often viewed with suspicion and their value was frequently questioned. There are many reasons for this but in my view the overarching reason was one of suspicion because of the approach. This often was interpreted as being anti- psychiatry.

The prevailing culture was very much one that viewed drugs as the cornerstone of treating mental illness and psychologists were often stereotyped as being anti-psychiatry. In some respects this was understandable. Psychiatrists, nurses and even social workers wore white coats. In the industrial units, nurses still wore uniforms and people who were not nurses wore brown coats. Hospital receptionists also wore uniforms, as of course did porters, domestics and other ancillary staff. Psychologists and psychotherapists not only came to work in civvies but the type of clothes they wore was often at odds with the conservative nature of hospital staff. The men often wore corduroy jackets, had cravats or open neck shirts and frequently sported beards. Many women wore floral dresses and had a much more colourful, some had an almost Bohemian, outlook on life. Their values were very different: often liberal-minded and associated with CND, or part of the emerging hippy culture. I know this will be seen as a generalisation but that's how it was. I enjoyed meeting and getting to know these colleagues. It opened up for me an entirely different dimension to the treatment and care of the mentally ill. Many of my colleagues were ex-service personnel and were quite reactionary to change. The Vietnam War, as I said earlier, was in full tilt and I, along with some other colleagues, went on a march to Grosvenor Square, the location of the American embassy, to protest against the war. This was greeted with horror by many staff. There was a consultant psychiatrist who was also a psychotherapist and was a supporter of the "Troops out "movement in relation to Northern Ireland and tried to get many of the Irish nurses to sign a petition against British involvement in Ireland. One of the amusing anecdotes was of a nurse who felt coerced into signing the petition but scribbled his name rendering it indecipherable!

The overriding view of suspicion of what was known as the psychosocial approach took years to change. This was unfortunate as there is no doubt that both approaches had their merit.

Chapter 8: My further training.

The placements to different wards and departments continued and my knowledge increased. I enjoyed learning about the different types of drugs that were used in psychiatry and prided myself by getting to know in detail every aspect of each drug. The types of conditions they were prescribed for, the range of dosages, their side effects, contra-indications, shapes, colours and so on.

I and other students used to constantly test each other on our knowledge. I loved studying. The generic term mental illness does not do justice to the complexity of the conditions and types of disorders. For example. Schizophrenia had a subset of types of schizophrenia: Hebephrenic, Chronic, Paranoid, Catatonic. Depression in those days were divided into "reactive"" where an event such as the loss of a loved one can cause depression or "endogenous". This is where someone is depressed and there are no obvious reasons as to why. Nowadays the thinking has moved on and these terms are not used.

Anatomy and physiology I found to be a joy. In my school education we were not taught about the human body. Within a year of my training I could name virtually every bone and muscle in the body, the cranial nerves, their names and functions, the structures and functions of the vital organs. Critics of mental health nurse training often said that too much emphasis was placed on aspects such as anatomy and physiology. I could not disagree more. I think it is vital that mental health nurses have an acute understanding of how the body functions. Many of the drugs used in psychiatry then and nowadays have as already mentioned have significant side effects. The new generation of atypical anti-psychotic drugs have significant side effects. Weight gain, particularly, is a consequence of anti-psychotic drugs. It is also worth commenting in 2024 that the life expectancy of people suffering from severe and enduring mental health illnesses is 20 years less than the general population. There has been a reappraisal of the education of mental health nurses in the UK with a much greater emphasis on the physical as well as the psychological needs of the mentally ill.

As with any occupation, most people that are keen to progress not only do well but, also, they gain more confidence. At the eighteen-month stage of my training I sat the intermediate examination. This consisted of a three-hour paper along traditional lines where candidates were given nine questions and asked to select six to answer. I along with the rest of my set was successful and we moved onto the next stage of our training. With my new-found confidence I felt much more able to engage with patients.

Chapter 9: The Visit

This led to me being more adventurous. One particular event sticks vividly in my mind.

The patient, Aubrey, I referred to earlier was still on the same long-stay ward when I was allocated there for a second time. We got to know each other well. He had long lost the vicious cycles of manic depression and was interesting to speak with. He in turn was keen to know about me and particularly why did I decide to train as a psychiatric nurse.

One afternoon we were sitting in the ward garden and he began to speak about his parents. He reminded me that his father was in the colonial service as it then was and had worked overseas. Aubrey was sent back to England to board at one of the leading public schools, as was common practice for people of that class in those days. He recounted how in his teenage years his illness developed and that how as a young man he had eventually been committed to a mental hospital. He spoke about his mother's distress and reflected on how difficult it must have been for them. After his father retired his parents lived in a small country town about twenty miles from the hospital. They visited him regularly but he was never well enough to be discharged. From reading his notes, it was quite evident that when in his manic phase he could create huge turmoil and was very difficult to handle. In his depressed phase he was incapable of caring for himself. This combined with the years of incarceration had damaged him. He had also received hundreds of ECT shocks plus years of anti-psychotic medication. Despite all of this and although in his 70's he was remarkably coherent and in fact good company. It was apparent to me that he was highly intelligent and that, had it not been for his illness, he would have succeeded well in life.

On this particular afternoon, he was maudlin about his parents and he asked me if he could visit their grave. He knew where they were buried and had in fact attended their funeral some thirty years earlier. Both his parents had died within a few months of each other and were buried in the same grave. I couldn't see any problem with it and I spoke with the charge nurse. This was one of those occasions when I encountered the worst side of the institutions. This charge nurse had a very custodial attitude and was dismissive of the idea. He said he could see little point in it and felt it that it was a waste of time. Unperturbed, I spoke with the charge nurse on the other shift who was warm to the idea. He was very familiar with Aubrey and had known him for many years. This charge nurse was coming up for retirement and spoke quite movingly about the tragedy of so many patients that he had nursed over the years. He had seen many of them grow old in hospital and understood the toll the years of institutionalisation had caused for so many people. The upshot was that I was given permission to take Aubrey to see his parents' grave. Once again there was the "madness" of the mental hospital system to contend with. First, the assistant chief male nurse said that I would have to go on my day off as he had no intention of giving me a day out for no good reason.

Again, just to digress, I played for the hospital football team, and we were regularly given time off to play other hospitals on a home and away basis, but to do something with an individual patient was seen as profligate. Undeterred I said I was happy to go on my day off. The shift system in hospitals meant that we all had significant leisure time, so it was not in any way a problem for me. I thought at one time I would have to pay my own bus fare; however, the supportive charge nurse sorted this for me and also arranged that we should take a packed lunch with us.

We set off and had to make two bus changes before arriving at the church. Aubrey was quiet most of the way and spent the journey looking out of the bus window. He had of course left the hospital on many occasions to go on outings but I think this had been the first time in half a century or more that he had been on public transport. I also considered that he might have been ruminating on his parents or what might life had been for him had he not been ill.

We eventually arrived at the church. Fortunately, it was a wonderful spring day. Daffodils and tulips were in abundance and the church grass had been freshly mown. Locating the grave was remarkably easy. I knew the dates of his parents' deaths from Aubrey's case notes and found the area of the cemetery where people of those years were buried. The interesting thing was that there was not an erect headstone but a stone with inscriptions set into the ground. The stone was marble and had not been cleaned in many a long year plus grass had encroached significantly onto the stone. We set about cleaning it up using a broom and watering can, which were made available by the vicar's wife and our bare hands. Working together, we quickly cleaned it up. After doing so, we paused to reflect on the grave. At this point Aubrey broke down, wept uncontrollably and fell to his knees. He spoke to the grave as though speaking to his parents: he apologised and said that he was sorry he caused them so much agony and heartache. He spoke about the despair they must have felt that their only child ended up in a mental hospital. He referred to them as Mama and Papa. It was genuinely touching. After a while, we moved to a bench where we sat and talked about his parents. We ate our lunch and eventually decided it was time to make our way back. We went back to the grave and stood there in silence for about five minutes.

It was at that moment that I noticed something. The gravestone obviously contained the names of his parents and their years of births and deaths. It was a high-quality piece of work; however, there was a significant gap at the bottom of the stone, enough to have the name and life years of another person. It occurred to me that his parents might have designed the stone with a view to Aubrey's being buried with them. It seemed improbable that such a significant gap would have been left on a stone that otherwise had been so professionally designed. I decided not to mention this to Aubrey. We travelled back in virtual silence but when we arrived at the hospital Aubrey shook hands with me and thanked me for taking him to see his parents' grave. I spoke with the charge nurse who had been supportive and mentioned the gravestone. We then went through Aubrey's case notes and there was no mention of any request from his parents that he be interred with them. The charge nurse advised that it was better to leave it there. Three months later, Aubrey died peacefully in his sleep. He was buried in the hospital graveyard and thus a life ended that had begun with such promise and was lived in such tragedy, turmoil and sadness. I felt privileged to have known him. Among other things I could not help about thinking of Aubrey's class mates from all those years ago. Many would have gone on to have had highly successful careers as the school in question has a reputation for producing scholar's, lawyers, doctors etc. and how unaware they would have been that Aubrey's life had taken such a different direction. I wondered as we were travelling on the bus through some leafy wealthy upmarket villages if we were passing by the houses of any of his school friends. The whole phenomena of ships in the night and how lives can take different directions was something that I pondered on for some time. I reflected on the vagaries of life and how devastating mental illness can be on the lives of individuals and their families.

Chapter 10: Relationships with medical staff.

Hospitals, I had discovered, were very hierarchical. So much depended on your status and not what you might be able to contribute.

A particular event comes to mind. On the locked ward, a man was admitted who was severely depressed and there were worries that he might be suicidal. He had no previous history of depression or mental illness. On arriving at the ward accompanied by his wife, he was indeed depressed and looked quite forlorn. His wife was distressed and could not stay on the ward as it was too upsetting for her. A junior doctor came to the ward to carry out the admission procedure. This involved a physical examination followed by a discussion. The doctor on this occasion was new to the hospital and to the UK. He had trained overseas and his English was very poor. I hasten to add that the NHS has recruited since the 1950's from overseas and these staff in a wide variety of roles have made a most valuable contribution to the Health Service specifically and to the British way of life more generally. However, this young doctor, probably newly qualified, was an example of a hospital desperately short of staff and employing someone whose knowledge of psychiatry was virtually nil and his ability to communicate highly compromised. In psychiatry the brain is the organ of access and to not be able to communicate with someone renders the physician virtually incapable of making sense of the problems the person has, let alone be in a position to help resolve them.

The depressed man was cooperative, the physical examination was carried out proficiently and there were no discernible physical health problems.

The conversation ensued. This consisted of this doctor going through a checklist. In fact, there was no conversation as such. The patient was asked about his marital status, his children, siblings, parents' mental and psychiatric history, his occupation, sleep pattern, diet, exercise, smoking and drinking. All the questions were answered in a minimalist way and did not throw any light on his current difficulties. However, the question about his drinking illustrates just how pointless the whole encounter was. When asked about his alcohol intake the patient replied "very little". As the doctor was about to go onto the next question the man interrupted him and said "We have a drop of rum in our coffee with our elevenses on a Saturday morning". In his fractured English, the doctor said 'You take rum in your coffee?" to which the patient replied, "With our elevenses on Saturdays", and the doctor wrote? Drink/alcohol problem. I intervened at this point to try to clarify what was being said. The doctor was not well-disposed to a student nurse attempting to clarify matters and the inappropriate entry was left in the case notes. Astonishingly, there was no discussion with the patient about why he was depressed.

I spoke with the charge nurse about this. He in turn invited the patient into his office and I was allowed to sit in on the discussion. Over the course of 30 minutes, the man revealed that he had been depressed for some time. He spoke about his domineering wife, his business difficulties and his sense of worthlessness. I noticed how skillful the charge nurse was, asking open-ended questions and speaking in a gentle tone. He made very few notes at the time. When the discussion came to an end, the charge nurse asked me to stay with the patient. He then wrote a comprehensive account of his discussion with the patient. The charge nurse was of the view that the patient was a high suicide risk. He summoned the junior doctor back to the ward and asked him to fill out a suicide caution card. This the doctor readily did.

A suicide caution card was a method of alerting the ward staff to the perceived risk of suicide and every member of staff on the ward had to sign it. The patient was then kept under continual observation.

Later in the afternoon, when the charge nurse was busy in

another part of the ward, I answered the phone. It was the consultant psychiatrist who was ultimately responsible for the patient. She asked me to read the notes made on admission of the patient. I proceeded to read the charge nurse's note, which gave a comprehensive account of the man's state of mind. The consultant said that she found it interesting, particularly the view that the man posed a suicide risk. She asked me which doctor had admitted the patient. I explained that I was reading the charge nurse's observations, to which the consultant said that she wanted to hear what the doctor who had checked the patient in had said. I in my innocent manner attempted to explain that the interview note by the doctor was telegraphic and didn't really have anything of significance to explain. This was met with quite an abrupt response and I was obliged to read out the notes that were not a patch on the charge nurse's observations. I then found myself, for the second time in a few hours, relaying another odd interaction to the charge nurse.

I then had another tutorial in understanding how the system works. The charge nurse explained that there was a pecking order and that, irrespective of the knowledge and experience of a nurse, the view of a doctor no matter how junior and inexperienced would always take precedence. We discussed how ridiculous this was but the charge nurse said "That's the way it is".

Later the consultant came to the ward and, after a discussion with the charge nurse and then interviewing the patient herself, she agreed that the patient was suicidal and to the continuation of the suicide caution card.

Chapter 11: NIGHT DUTY

During the three-year training, students spent three months on night duty each year. This was a most unproductive time as it meant spending the night sitting in the semi-darkness with a dormitory full of patients who were asleep. Virtually every patient was on some form of night sedation and therefore the patients slept through the night. The most common drugs were a barbiturate, sodium amytal and paraldehyde a powerful tranquiliser that was highly addictive.

I spent the monotonous hours reading and like most of the staff trying to stay awake.

Third year student nurses often took charge of wards at night. The wards we were in charge of were the long-stay wards. The acute admission wards and locked wards, where there were more disturbed and challenging patients, were staffed by several nurses with a registered nurse always in charge. At the time we thought nothing of students taking charge of wards. Looking back, it seems such a huge responsibility for 20-year-olds, but that is how it was.

Some of the outlying wards in the hospital known as Villas were unstaffed. The patients were locked in at night and it was one of the duties of student nurses to check the villas three times during the night. Most of us found this quite scary as it entailed going out into the grounds alone and then walking through the wards, which were big, eerie, dark, and then up to the dormitories. Whilst most of these rounds were uneventful, you could never be sure what you might find. Occasionally there might be a patient in a disturbed state; sometimes a patient feeling unwell; and occasionally a patient might be dead in bed. This was discovered as you were expected to walk through the dormitories stopping to check if each patient was breathing. Very occasionally a patient might have committed suicide, hanging being the most common method. Quite traumatic for a 20-year-old to discover.

The first time I discovered a person who had died of suicide was when I was working night duty on an acute admission ward. It was quite early into our night shift when a patient had accidentally upset a jug of water. I went into the sluice room to get a mop and bucket. In the half-light after getting the bucket, I turned around and bumped into the feet of a man hanging from the ceiling. I was taken aback and to this day I can recall vividly how my heart raced and I was full of fear. I quickly called the staff nurse and between the two of us we tried to lift the hanging body so as to relieve the pressure on the man's neck but to no avail. He was already dead and the weight of a hanging person is such that it was difficult to lift him.

Eventually with the help of other staff, we cut him down but it was clear he had been dead for some time. The police were called and the Coroner's officer took statements, In those days there was no inquiry as such, although the next day the staff who were on duty in the afternoon were all interviewed as it was during their shift that the patient hanged himself.

The mentality was that this is the sort of thing that happens, albeit quite rarely.

As for the staff, there was very little in terms of support. There was a macho culture and you were expected to just get on with life.

One other thing that comes to mind during one of my night duty stints was when working on the locked ward.

As with the other wards because the patients were on night sedation most slept through the night. Occasionally there might be a patient who was bi-polar and might be so high that he could not settle and in these cases they were then nursed in a side room or very occasionally in the padded cell, colloquially known as "The Pad".

Many of the wards have problems with rats. At night on the locked ward you could frequently hear them gnawing away under the floor boards. I was working with a staff nurse who increasingly became irritated and disconcerted by the noise. I didn't feel to good about it either and in the dormitory where we sat we put or feet up on chairs, as it had been known that occasionally a rat may come through one of the gaps in the floor boards. On one particular night the rats were very active. John the nurse in charge eventually decided that this had to stop, and he went into the clinic room and retrieved a large bottle of sodium amytal capsules a very powerful barbiturate that has sedative-hypnotic properties.

John broke up several dozen of the capsules and mixed them with bread and milk and Largactil syrup. He then proceeded to push the mixture through the cracks of the floorboards where we could hear most of the gnawing.

The gnawing actually increased for quite some while and John put this down to more rats being attracted because of the mixture. After several hours the gnawing stopped.

Many months later the heating system in the ward was being replaced and the heating engineers on removing the floorboards were shocked to discover a huge number of dead rats. It became the talk of the hospital.

By his time I was back on day duty and I received a phone call from John who was in an agitated state imploring me not to say anything to anyone about his actions, which of course I did not.

In those days the scrutiny on drugs was very limited and the fact that he could use such a large amount of sodium amytal and Largactil syrup and go unnoticed says much about the amount of sedation that was used. Hopefully it could not happen nowadays.

Chapter 12: Boundaries

It was made clear during our training that it was not appropriate to disclose personal information to patients even if the intentions were well meaning.

There was an incident with a student nurse and a highly complex patient that could have had a catastrophic outcome.

The patient was a highly successful businessman. Well-educated and, on first meeting him, it was difficult to understand why he was in hospital. However, he was a highly complex individual who had become embroiled in a fraudulent enterprise and had been initially awaiting trial but, due to his mental state, he was considered not fit to stand trial and was sectioned. He also gained some national notoriety as, when he was on the run from the police, he appeared on the front page of a national newspaper pointing at the Torrey Canyon, an oil tanker that ran aground off the west coast of Cornwall in March 1967 spilling thousands of tons of oils onto the beaches and devastating the marine life. Some of the staff at the hospital were of the view that he was faking his condition as a means of exculpating himself from the criminal proceedings. Many others did not.

This man suffered from a paranoid disorder.

A student nurse who was Canadian was allocated to the locked ward during my allocation. He was a lively individual and might be described as someone who was trying to 'walk before he could run'. In his briefing by the charge nurse, he was quite fascinated by this man's history and, despite having been warned that this man should be treated with a high degree of caution, the very first afternoon on the ward he spent a long time in the courtyard speaking with him.

We were to discover that in conversation the patient had stated that MI5 were out to kill him and that they had managed to poison some cigarettes that his wife had given him. Our Canadian student assured him that this could not be the case and demonstrated this by offering to smoke one of the cigarettes, which he did. This convinced the patient that the student nurse was part of the conspiracy and that he had immunity from the poison. The student had also disclosed a significant amount of personal information about his family life in Canada. He said he had done this to somehow get across to the patient that he was a 'regular guy' and that, by disclosing personal Information, it would generate trust and in turn he would be able to help the patient. The opposite was the case. That night the patient who was very persuasive asked another patient who was easily influenced to kill the student. He convinced this patient that the student nurse was out to harm several of the patients and he also promised the patient some considerable financial reward for carrying out the deed.

The plot was only uncovered when the patient was overheard sharing the plan with another patient.

It was interesting that, when confronted, the patient readily admitted that he had commissioned the other patient to carry out the deed. I was present when the charge nurse asked him about this. He was unrepentant, simply explaining that the nurse was an MI5 plant who had wanted to harm him and that he was protecting himself. The cold and unemotional manner in his response was chilling and reinforced to me just how dangerous paranoid people can be. The student was transferred to another ward. A chastening lesson to all involved.

Chapter 13: An unpleasant encounter.

During one of my placements, I was asked by one of the assistant chief male nurses to spend a few days on another ward as they had a high rate of sickness and were short of staff. This I readily agreed to although in reality, despite the courtesy of being asked, I didn't have a choice.

These few days turned out to be some of the most unpleasant and disagreeable in my training. The charge nurse of the ward was on annual leave and the regular staff nurse of the ward was in charge. He was quite surly in his attitude to me right from the start. I had no idea why, as we had never met before. Everything I did seemed to be either wrong or was sneered at. For example, he asked me to get a roll of sleek from the clinical room. Sleek was a form of sticking plaster used to adhere dressings to pressure sores. I had never used or heard of sleek as, on the ward I had been on, we used micropore that had just come onto the market. When I asked him what sleek was, he belittled me, saying how could someone not know what it was. This may sound trivial but on top of a never-ending stream of comments it was becoming a bit wearing. In those days, you were expected to endure it; there was certainly no question of raising a grievance or complaining about bullying or harassment. Things came to a head on a Sunday afternoon. It was a sunny day and, as with every Sunday, the local band of the Salvation Army toured the hospital grounds stopping outside many wards playing for the patients. We had placed a number of the patients, most in geriatric chairs, in the ward garden. This had a high fence and hedges so it was not possible to see over the hedge. I noticed that a number of the patients became animated when they heard the band, some tapping their feet or hands and others looking up inquisitively. I unlocked the gate of the garden and invited the band in, which they were delighted to do.

The patients were enjoying the music when the staff nurse came out and in a very intemperate manner asked who let the band in. I explained it was me and I went on to say how and how much the patients were enjoying it. As soon as the band finished their last piece, he asked them to leave. He then confronted me in an aggressive manner wanting to know who did I think I was making that kind of decision without permission. I responded by saying that I thought it was bizarre that some elderly people could not have the pleasure of a few minutes of enjoyment. I went on to ask him why he was in this job and suggested he lacked any warmth or empathy for the patients. He, in turn, asked me if I was a homosexual, which took me aback. He went on to say that he couldn't stand people with long hair and he would be glad when I went back to my own ward. I asked him if he had a problem with his sexuality because of his comment. I also said it seemed really weird that his comment was prompted by me allowing a few patients to enjoy some music. He then threatened to punch me in the mouth. I replied saying that if he did I would call the police. He seemed bemused by this and I added that just how institutionalised he was in assuming that working in a mental hospital somehow insulated him from the normal considerations in mainstream life. Needless to say, the next few days were tortuous and I was pleased to be out of there. The interesting thing about this man was that on one hand he was not overtly cruel to the patients but he had no empathy or warmth. The job was simply a routine. "Get them up, wash, dress, feed, administer medication, keep everyone in order". As for the homosexual comment, I've learned over the years that people who have unresolved issues over their sexuality are the ones most likely to be homophobic, as they need to constantly reassure themselves or others about themselves.

Even though this encounter was many years ago, I recall it as vividly today as when it happened. I'm sure there must have been many students and perhaps others that had an equally unsatisfactory experience and some students may have discontinued their training. Little wonder there was a high level of sickness when this man was in charge!

Nowadays we hear a lot about bullying and harassment. Certainly in those days there was a much harsher culture and as with many aspects of the working life in mental hospitals there was an expectation that when there were difficulties you simply sucked it up and got on with it. In a perverse way it did instil some resilience to me and helped me develop a skill set in how to cope in challenging circumstances.

And so my training continued.

Chapter 14: The Female side.

Although the hospital was divided between what was known as the male and female sides, male students were seconded to the female side for three months in their three-year training and vice versa.

The ward to which I was allocated was an acute admission ward. The patients were seriously ill but were not violent. These patients had depression, anxiety disorders, phobias, bi-polar and a range of psychotic illnesses but not presenting in an aggressive or disturbed manner. It was this ward where in addition to the usual medication, insulin therapy was used alongside ECT for depression.

This was one of the most enjoyable placements in my training. The ward sister was Irish and she set very high standards. She was a great teacher and I learnt a huge amount from her. The consultant psychiatrist was a man who could be temperamental, but this ward sister knew how to handle him and, by observing her techniques, I again was lucky to have such a good role model. She was strict but not punitive with the staff and enjoyed huge respect. The patients on this ward did really well despite the complexity of their conditions. One of the most notable aspects that I learnt in my placement was the deployment of 'soft skills' by female nurses. These were interventions and approaches to patients using a non-judgemental and a more empathetic approach. That's not to say that male nurses were the opposite; it was more about the emphasis. As a result, there was far less tension on the ward. This may sound obvious but the contrast was profound and had I not had the exposure to this approach I might not have developed the skills that were to stand me in good stead throughout my career. The interesting thing for me was that the reputation of the sister that went before her with some male nurses was not a complimentary one. This I found strange because my experience was so positive. We got on really well and on my last day on the ward she said how much she had enjoyed having me on her ward. I've never forgotten her and consider myself fortunate to have had the opportunity to work with her. As for her reputation, I can only put it down to the fact that by setting high standards she may not have endeared herself to some, she certainly did to me.

Chapter 15: The management of the hospital.

In those days hospitals were managed by what was known as HMC's. (Hospital Management Committees).

These consisted of a hospital secretary (CEO) in today's terms, a matron, chief male nurse and an independent chair and lay members. Although over the years there have been countless re-organisations and titles, the structure in real terms remains very much the same.

As with any administration, they were hugely variable in their approach and effectiveness. The chief male nurse (CMN) at my hospital was not a bad person in any way but his management style was to be aloof. He obviously thought this was the way to conduct himself, so if, for example, you passed him on a hospital corridor and said good morning he ignored you. There was no talk of motivation or any sense of staff involvement to generate new ideas or to seek out views on how to improve things. I once wrote to the CMN suggesting some ideas and to my shock I was asked to come and meet with him. My fellow students thought I was in for a dressing down; however, to my surprise, he was interested in my ideas and thanked me for writing to him. This reaction was not what I expected and it was only years later that I worked out that he was a shy man and his way of coping was to create some distance. There were other managers such as deputy and assistant CMN's who were very positive; others not so.

The matron truly did rule with a rod of iron. I find it amusing when people talk about bringing back matrons. This is unrealistic. In those days the matron and CMN were in loco parentis over students as the age of majority was 21. The employment laws and rights of individuals were not as they are today and the autocratic approach would not be allowed. The matron of our hospital was a benevolent dictator and most of the time seemed to get it right. The difficulty came when anyone challenged the system; even if the challenge was positive, they were put down in no uncertain terms.

Finance was never mentioned; it was simply assumed that there was a bottomless pit of money. Although the memory fades for many people, the mental hospitals were very cheap to run. A long-stay ward of 40 patients who were compliant and run often by one nurse on duty was highly cost effective.

And so my training continued with a range of placements culminating in my final exams, all of which I passed.

There is one anecdote from my viva that I will share. The viva was a 30-minute question and answer session when you were asked about specific issues such as to explain a particular section of the Mental Health Act or the side effect of a drug. You were also given a scenario and asked to comment on how you would handle it. The consultant psychiatrist asked me how I would react if, during visiting times, a patient upset a tray of tea. I answered that the first thing is not assume that it was an act of aggression but that it might be an accident. Before I could say any more, the consultant interrupted me and said, "Thank God for that. I've asked this question before, and the response has always been along the lines of assuming that this is an act of aggression. Your's, Carter, is the response I've been longing for."

To digress; this was an issue, all those years ago and is still today that far too often people pathologize normal reactions to events. A patient looks a bit down or is fed up and it is turned into a medical condition. A patient is upset with how another patient or staff member has spoken to them and it is assumed to be a manifestation of their illness.

I will not be bashful. I was thrilled with the reaction of the consultant who said he had no further questions for me.

I enjoyed the course and at the end felt lucky to have by accident found an occupation that I enjoyed and was fulfilling.

Chapter 16: The Hermit.

Writing this piece has reminded me of another example that personifies how people, however well-meaning can also treat those with mental illness in way that perplexes me.

One of the hospitals I worked at was deep in the countryside. There was a man who was mentally ill but not a patient of ours, he lived as a hermit. Some of us presumed he lived in the extensive woods that surrounded the hospital, but others thought he used to travel miles away as he had occasionally been spotted in distant towns. This man had developed an affinity with one of the charge nurses, Frank, and he used to turn up at the hospital once in a while. He was always absolutely filthy. Hair and beard long and matted, clothes caked in mud and filth. His nails were long and he was emaciated. He used to present at one of the doors of the ward that looked out onto the woods. We worked out that it was not an accident that he would always arrive when this charge nurse was on duty, he would wait in the woods until he saw Frank arriving for work. Frank would let him in and immediately take him to the bathroom. His clothes were deposited into a linen bag for incineration and our hermit would go straight into a hot bath. He was deloused and the hospital barber would come to the ward to shave his head and beard off. Over the next day the chiropodist would sort out the overgrown nails and he would be given a through physical examination. We always remarked that his teeth were in remarkably good order. He would stay for a few days, occasionally for over a week. He was quiet and thoughtful, very polite and would sleep well. Eventually he would say to Frank that he would be moving on. Frank would prepare a bag full of food, sandwiches, cake, fruit and a flask of tea. He was kitted out in new clothes an overcoat and new shoes. Our hermit friend would say good-bye and then disappear into the woods. He was often not seen again for six to nine months. He was diagnosed with a schizoaffective disorder and this was the way he (harmlessly) lived his life. The consultant psychiatrist of the ward and Frank would suggest to him that he might wish to stay at the hospital and this he always declined. The general manager of the hospital, Cambridge educated, became aware of this and questioned why we were accommodating this man and thought it should be the responsibility of social services. A tortuous series of discussions ensued with the charge nurse and me at a loss to understand the mentality of this manager who was caught up with budgets and service level agreements. Oblivious to the fact that to occasionally care for the hermit, which cost very little, was providing a service to a person who needed support and care and was the humanitarian and compassionate thing to do. There was no way our hermit would engage with social services and this was the most effective way of supporting him. This type of short-sighted blinkered thinking at times beggars belief.

I occasionally cast my mind back and wondered what became of the hermit after the hospital closed.

Chapter 17: John and Elizabeth's story.

In 1997 at a mental hospital which as CEO of an NHS Trust came under my jurisdiction, there was a shocking incident that brings into sharp relief the need to be ever vigilant and aware that people who are vulnerable can be the subject of appalling abuse and that the processes and the system can mitigate against the perpetrators being held to account.

On an autumn morning a 46-year-old man, John, who had been a patient in the hospital for many years went into the hospital shop in a distressed state and told the two shop assistants that a male nurse had been cruel to him. John showed them his injuries, which shocked the women. They immediately informed the hospital manager who went to the shop and on seeing the injuries dialled 999 and John was taken by ambulance to the local general hospital. As soon as I was informed, I asked a senior and experienced manager to go to the hospital and commence an investigation.

The manager first went to the shop and interviewed the two shop assistants. He then went to the ward. He spoke with the charge nurse and asked him if anything untoward had occurred on the ward that morning to which he replied no. He then interviewed each of the nurses and the ward domestic all of whom confirmed that nothing out of the ordinary had happened that morning.

He then began to interview the patients on the ward who like the staff said that they had not seen anything of concern.

He was nearing the end of his interviews with the patients when he met with Elizabeth.

Elizabeth was in her mid-seventies and had been in hospital for over 40 years. She suffered from schizophrenia and during her interview with the manager was deluded and was hallucinating. She said that she could see Adolf Hitler and Hermann Goering in the room. The manager (as with the other people he had interviewed) was very careful not to describe the incident or make reference to the fact that John had been injured and was now in the A&E of the local hospital. In response to his question about whether anything had happened in the ward that morning Elizabeth gave a very descriptive account of her morning commencing from the time she woke up to going to the loo and having her breakfast. Towards the end of her account she said "Oh and I saw the nurse dragging John across the ward". When asked to describe in further detail what she had seen Elizabeth gave an account very similar to that of John.

The account was that John had become angry on refusing to leave the ward to go to one of the therapy departments he lay on the floor. The charge nurse took him by the ankles and dragged him the length of the ward. The injures that had so shocked the shop assistants and the manager was that the skin on his back from the waistline to his shoulders had been ripped off.

On further questioning, Elizabeth was adamant that this is what she had seen.

In parallel with the investigation, I had arranged for a psychiatrist to go to the general hospital to speak with John. The psychiatrist reached the conclusion that John was telling the truth about the incident, in fact his words were when I spoke with him were "I only wish I didn't believe him"

The charge nurse was re-interviewed by the manager and was asked if he could explain how the patient could have sustained his injuries. His explanation was that he believed they were self-inflicted by the patient scraping his back down the steps of the ward. He was asked why he hadn't mentioned this when first interviewed or if he had seen this happening why didn't do anything about it. The nurse replied that he hadn't realised the injuries were that severe. In terms of why would the patient inflict these injuries he replied that the patient was angry because he had asked him to leave the ward to go to a therapy unit which he was reluctant to do.

When this was reported back to me, I spoke with the consultant in the A&E department at the general hospital where the patient was being treated and asked him if it was plausible that the injuries could be self-inflicted to which he replied that he thought it was not possible.

We then considered what we had before us.

A patient with serious injuries alleging that the charge nurse of his ward had inflicted it by dragging him along the length of the ward.

There was Elizabeth who despite her schizophrenia gave a coherent account of the incident broadly similar to that of John.

A psychiatrist who had no previous knowledge of John believed John was telling him the truth.

A consultant in emergency medicine who did not think it plausible that the injuries had been self-inflicted.

We called the police who after interviewing the two patients were of the opinion that due to their psychiatric illnesses it was highly improbable that a conviction would be secured.

The charge nurse was suspended and in due course a disciplinary hearing was convened. In addition to John, Elizabeth gave evidence and both were consistent with their account of what had transpired. The union official representing the nurse was incredulous that we're taking into account the evidence of Elizabeth. Because we believed that the patients were telling us the truth the nurse was dismissed. We were taken to an employment tribunal on the grounds of unfair dismissal.

As with the disciplinary hearing the main line of criticism by the union representing the nurse was that our decision was unsafe as we had relied on the evidence of two patients, one of whom, Elizabeth was suffering from delusions and hallucinations and that even during the disciplinary hearing at she said she could see Hitler and Goering in the room.

Our case was that we had two people giving a coherent and consistent account of what had happened. We had gone through a robust investigation process that included getting an independent psychiatric opinion on John's veracity and that of the consultant at the general hospital who confirmed that the was not plausible that such serious injuries could have been self-inflicted. I had decided that we should not put Elizabeth or John through the ordeal of the employment Tribunal, rather we should rely on the fact that we had a proper process that would fulfil the requirements of the Tribunal.

When I was cross examined by the solicitor engaged by

the Union representing the nurse, in response to the allegation that it was unsafe to have relied on the evidence of Elizabeth, I made the point that although someone may have a major mental illness it doesn't mean the person is unreliable or that they are lying.

Needless to say, we were delighted when we received the judgement that our actions were unanimously up-held by the Tribunal. In their judgment they emphasised that we had conducted a thorough investigation and the fact two of the people had a mental illness was not a relevant factor.

Following this outcome, I spoke with people at the Department of Health as I thought this was something that should have been shared more widely. It was a commonly held view at that time that allegations in which the only witnesses were people who were mentally ill would not stand up to the test of a fair process if challenged in court or at a Tribunal. It was very disappointing when there was no appetite to publicise the outcome more widely.

Chapter 18: A morning with a Community Psychiatric Nurse (CPN)

In my work at the Royal College of Nursing I made a point each week of spending time in a clinical service. This was part of the work that was so enjoyable. Over the years at the RCN I went all over the UK and witnessed at first hand the work of some amazing nurses.

A visit that sticks in my mind so vividly is one when I spent a morning with a CPN. It was pre-arranged so that the patients could be consulted in advance that they were happy for the nurse to be accompanied by me. Three visits to patient homes were arranged.

One of the visits was to a man in his 50's who had a diagnosis of chronic schizophrenia. On arriving at his flat after introducing me, the CPN immediately asked the him to sort out his laundry and they put the first load into the washing machine. She the looked in his fridge and talked through with him what he had been eating. We then got into her car and drove to a local supermarket. The nurse helped the man choose a selection of food including fruit and fresh vegetables. She was later to explain to me that if the fruit and veg were bought he would eat it.

On returning to the flat we had a cup of tea and a chat. All the time the CPN was assessing the patient and we eventually got to the point where she took him into the bedroom and administered his depot injection.

I thanked him for allowing me to be come and meet him and he quite spontaneously told me how well supported he was by his nurse and that it had been many years since he had been admitted back to hospital. I also notice that physically he looked well as was his personal hygiene. This is important to note because people with severe and enduring mental health problems often suffer from very poor physical health and neglect themselves. Consequently, as already mentioned they often have a life expectancy of 20 years less than the average person in the UK.

There are a number of reasons for this. Poor lifestyle in terms of diet, little exercise, smoking and many of the drugs to treat severe and enduring mental illness can cause obesity and thus increasing cardiovascular disease.

When the CPN and I returned to her car she asked me if she could speak to me in confidence. She knew that in the afternoon I was meeting with members of the Board of the Trust. She asked me not to mention that she had taken the patient to the supermarket and had helped him with his laundry etc. I was astonished as this is exactly what I thought a CPN should be doing. I was very complimentary about her interactions with the patient and that she was taking care of the whole person and not simply administering his depot injection. The CPN explained that her managers would suggest that the domestic issues should be the responsibility of social services and not the NHS. She thought that the view of managers would also be that the role of the nurse is to administer the depot injections and that if she had time to take the patient to the supermarket etc. this time would be better spent taking on more patients to her case load and concentrate on administering depots. How accurate this is I'm not sure and equally I'm know there are plenty of managers who would not hold this view. Nevertheless this was the concern of this highly credible and immensely talented nurse.

If this is the case it's another example of some of those in authority simply not understanding the nature of mental illness and how best to care for people.

Chapter 19: My Career

I do not intend to dilate too much on my career but, after qualifying, I had a range of clinical experience ranging from working as a staff nurse on a locked ward, geriatric, children and adolescents and adult acute wards. I undertook further training in family and group therapy and for a while had a small caseload of people living in the community; this was when I worked in a psychiatric unit in a general hospital. I enjoyed all of these jobs, each of which gave me grounding for my career, which ended as a CEO of a large NHS Trust in London, which I did for 12 years. It was a hugely enjoyable job; however, I believe many of the principles of my approach to management were forged by the roles models and experience that I had in my nurse training.

I then had nine very happy years at the Royal College of Nursing

Of course, there were challenges in both jobs but they both were enormously fulfilling.

In writing this book I shared the drafts with several people and whilst all were encouraging and made helpful comments most of which I have taken on board, one of the people who gave me some detailed advice was Professor Peter Tyrer Emeritus Professor at Imperial

College.

Peter felt there had to be a stronger link between the first part of the book which is an account of my journey through nurse training in a psychiatric hospital and the second part of the book which is about my concern over the state of mental health services in the UK and the failure to properly plan the transition from the old mental hospitals to the model we have today.

I have accepted his comments and in doing so it seems sensible to signpost at this point in the book as I have already alluded to, that I have misgivings over the wholesale closure and running down of most of the UK's mental hospitals. The following chapters outline my reasons for holding this view.

Chapter 20: The closure of the mental hospitals.

I wish to stress that what I am about to write is not a call to rebuild mental hospitals; far from it, but it is an attempt to give my opinion why things went wrong and how, in my view, we have a far inferior mental health system than we would have if there had been a more thoughtful way of changing mental health care across the country.

I have commented on the Ely hospital inquiry. In addition, from the late 60's in to the 1970's there were a series of inquiries and investigations into other hospitals. Two of the highest profile of were:

Whittingham Hospital, near Preston in Lancashire and St Augustine's Hospital in Kent, both now closed, where abuse took place on a massive scale.

There were in total 23 mental hospital inquiries.

Each of these inquiries attracted high profile comment in the national press and on radio and television. The findings were consistent highlighting institutional practices.

The net effect was an assumption that all mental hospitals were badly managed and that abuse and neglect were the order of the day combined with a disregard for the human rights of patients, overseen by psychiatrists who were only keen on drugging up patients or zapping them with ECT.

This is simply not true. I saw countless examples of compassionate care and psychiatrists doing their absolute best to minimise levels of medication and to be at the forefront of heralding in a more enlightened approach to their clinical practice.

The emergence of community-based practice gathered pace in the 1970's, aided by the on-going emergence of more effective anti-psychotic drugs, particularly depot injections. The drug Modecate was one of the first of this genre to emerge. It was, as has already been mentioned in this book, one of the antipsychotic drugs that is prepared in a thick oily substance and is injected deep into the gluteus muscle of the buttock and then is slowly released over several weeks depending on the dose. This obviates the need for patients to have to remember to self-medicate several times a day and was a major factor in helping people to stay well and out of hospital. Also, at this time there was the emergence of more occupational therapy and an increase in music therapy, art and other creative therapies. Occupancy rates in hospitals were falling as a result of these interventions as were lengths of stay.

The bad publicity over poor standards of care coupled with the anti-psychiatry movement and "Mind" were however in the forefront of the closure programme.

The emphasis was on closure and not on re-provision.

The pace of closure increased in the 1980's and continued into the 1990's. It became a badge of honour for senior managers to claim the accolade for closing a hospital. Frequently people would say "I closed such and such a hospital". Rarely was the expression used "I have re-provided alternative smaller-based services for people who will have a need for some form of residential care either short- or long-term".

The huge estates were sold off and the proceeds swallowed up by the Treasury. A fraction was put into the funding of new locally based facilities.

To convert this for the reader into reality I will give the following example. Horton Hospital in Epsom was opened in 1902 and was due for final closure in the late 1990's.

The catchment area for Horton was the London Borough of Westminster. Although a borough associated with the Houses of Parliament, Buckingham Palace and the West End, Westminster has a large resident population and in Victorian times the mental hospitals were built on the outskirts of our large cities thus providing farmland and space for the residents. Therefore, for over a hundred years right up until the 1990's, people from Westminster who were mentally ill went to Horton. As each mental hospital was closed, the reprovision was back in the Borough or town from where people originated.

This led to confusion with the public and the media, as people would question why are all these people being brought into this borough and there was often resistance to the development of mental health residential units, with the result that general hospital sites were often used. In addition, many of the patients might have been in hospital for many decades and were now coming back to an area where they had long lost touch with any relatives or friends. Therefore, there was the conundrum of where to house these patients.

For those who know Vauxhall Bridge Road in the London Borough of Westminster they will be aware that it is one of the busiest thoroughfares in London. Each hour thousands of cars and lorries drive along it. Most people travelling through will not notice a large uninspiring building, which is the Gordon Hospital. This hospital was opened in 1884 as was originally known as the Western Hospital for fistula, piles and other diseases of the rectum. It was renamed in 1886 in honour of Major General Charles Gordon otherwise known as Gordon of

Khartoum.

It came into the NHS in 1947 as part of the Westminster group of hospitals. These hospitals closed in 1992. It was surplus to requirements as the services had transferred into the newly built Chelsea and Westminster Hospital. In addition, it was not fit for purpose as, due to its age, it could not accommodate the equipment and associated facilities needed in a modern general hospital. There it stood in a dilapidated state surplus to requirements. The decision was made to use the Gordon for people who were acutely mentally ill requiring admission to hospital. It was a cheap way of re-providing the services that would be needed as a result of the closure of the Horton Hospital in Epsom.

Just pause for thought: people were being brought into the Gordon where there was no outdoor space (other than a cage erected on the roof) on one of the busiest thoroughfares in the country, into a run-down Victorian hospital that was not fit for purpose, and this was deemed to be progress. How absurd. At the time of writing the Gordon is finally due to be closed but it was for many patients over the past three decades the most un-therapeutic environment in which to be admitted.

A second example, and believe me there are countless others, was in relation to the closure of Shenley in

Hertfordshire.

This hospital, built on the outskirts of London, served the London Boroughs of Brent and Harrow. On the campus at the Central Middlesex, Brent, there was a plot of land that had lain barren for many years. The North West Thames Regional Health Authority decided that a psychiatric unit should be built there, thus bringing the service back to the heart of the catchment area, so far so good.

This was in the late 80's and, at that time, the financial state of the UK was precarious. As a result, the then Brent and Harrow Health Authority decided that they couldn't afford to commission a new design for a psychiatric unit and therefore took an off-the-shelf design for a unit that was designed in 1970. This was known as the racetrack design and consisted of six-bedded dormitories. The design had long been consigned to the past and was not fit for purpose for the latter part of the 20th century. Despite this, the then managers accepted this edict and a new building was constructed using an out-dated and discredited design. This coupled with being cramped on the edge of a large general hospital with poor recreation space could not in any way been deemed as progress. Quite the opposite: as un-therapeutic an environment as you could imagine. It is worth stating at this stage that, over the years, the clinical staff at both the Gordon and

Central Middlesex have done an amazing job under the most taxing of conditions. It didn't have to be like this. Both the Horton and Shenley sites cover over several hundred acres and are now upmarket housing developments. Some of the capital receipts from the sale of these properties should have been ploughed back into the re-provision. It was an opportunity to build high-quality facilities. Progress; I think not.

A further example of how the capital resources from the mental hospital closures relates to Banstead, a large mental hospital on the outskirts of Epsom. The money realised from the sale was used to build an underground car park at the Charing Cross Hospital. Not a penny invested in mental health services.

The need to accelerate the closure programme also resulted in shocking scandals that treated people with severe and enduring mental illness like disposable commodities. The *Sutton Guardian* revealed in an article headlined *'Friendless, Forlorn…Forgotten'* that exposed the plight of ex-Banstead patients consigned to 84 Hastings boarding houses, without the Riverside District Health Authority even informing the local social services or health authority.

At St Bernard's Hospital in Ealing 120 patients were discharged in the course of just 11 months to 28 different places scattered far and wide across the Home Counties and as far afield as Lytham St Anne's on the North West Coast. As with Banstead the transfer of these patients was done in stealth without the social services or the health authority in Lytham or other areas being alerted. This prompted an inquiry by the then North West Thames Regional Health Authority which resulted in criticising the transfer as nothing more than 'dumping' people long distances without any provision for infrastructure or support. Quite aside from the fact that areas such as Blackpool were already struggling to cope with their own challenges caring for people who were mentally ill. It was symptomatic of a closure programme that was based on financial need and had little to do with caring for people who deserved so much more. There are countless further examples of this abject failure to properly plan for the post Hospital era. Despite these lamentable failures the people responsible were rarely held to account it was often swept away with the phrase "There are lessons to be learnt from this".

"Care in the community" I think not, "Neglect in the community" would be more accurate.

Chapter 21: Horton Hospital Epsom

I became the chief executive of what at that time was known as the Northwest London Mental Health Trust in 1995.

In 1997, talks commenced with a number of NHS Trusts and their respective Health Authorities on a reconfiguration of mental health services across north, west and central London. The genesis of the need to review the number of Trusts emanates from the late 1980's into the 1990's.

With the creation of the internal market in the NHS, the view was that the market would drive up efficiency and drive down costs. It was devised on the business model of competitiveness designed to sweep aside any sense of complacency by providers. The strongly held view by many politicians and think tanks was that the NHS was inefficient and lacked the drive, agility and entrepreneurism to create a dynamic forward-thinking health service that at the same time was cost-effective and delivering value for money for the public.

However, as we were nearing the latter part of the 1990's, it was apparent that too many Trusts had been created and far from driving up efficiency there was waste, inefficiency and the management overheads of so many Boards of Directors and associated support could not be justified. In addition, there was a lack of coordination of services leading to fragmentation and, as previously discussed, mentally ill people falling between gaps in the service resulting in homicides, suicides and other serious incidents.

I and a colleague Pauline Ford, CEO of the neighbouring West London Mental Health Trust, drew up a plan proposing the merger of a number of Trusts and the absorption of services from some other Trusts who were providing mental health services.

These plans were readily endorsed by the Health Authorities within which the services were located but were met with huge resistance by some of the other NHS provider Trusts. Over the course of several months, discussions were held and eventually the decision was made to support the proposals devised by Pauline and myself to create two large Mental Health Trusts covering 8 London Boroughs. This meant the dissolution of NWL and the Riverside Mental Health Trust to create Brent Kensington & Chelsea NHS Trust (BKCW) that was eventuality to become the Central & North West London NHS Trust. The other Trust that absorbed some of the Riverside services retained the name West London Mental Health NHS Trust.

The CEOs' of the Trusts that were to be disbanded had to compete for the two jobs of the new Trusts and I was delighted to have been appointed CEO of the newly established BKCW Trust.

Within the portfolio of the services for which I was now

responsible was a unit known as the 'Horton Haven'. This consisted of a service for 75 people all of whom were long- stay patients at what remained of the old Horton mental hospital in Epsom.

Horton, a Victorian mental hospital, had been running down for many years and by the mid 90's only 75 patients remained. These were people suffering from severe and enduring mental illness and who had been in Horton for many years. Some were now quite elderly and the plan was to leave them all at Horton until they died or, as they became more frail and infirm, to transfer them to nursing homes. There were others who were younger and had complex problems and it was difficult to find places for them in the community

It was renamed 'Horton Haven' as that is exactly what it was. A haven for people who could not be transferred to community-based facilities and also did not need to be in an acute or locked mental health unit.

During the period when I was merging the two Trusts and arranging to absorb services from some other Trusts, I was surprised how unenthusiastic some of the senior managers from the Riverside NHS Trust were about Horton. When I eventfully visited Horton I was pleasantly surprised. Far from the image that had been portrayed as a service running down that few at head office wanted to manage, I came across an oasis of care and compassion. The 75 patients were well cared for and there was an enthusiastic team of staff that were a credit to the service.

The campus consisted of two wards remaining from the old hospital plus a former staff residence and a social centre. It was a hive of activity and creativity.

Adjacent to this complex were two empty wards. Horton was set in a few acres and had ample recreation space and the trees and bushes from the old hospital remained, thus leaving the most pleasing of surroundings.

On the edge of the campus was an old dilapidated house that had once been the residence of the medical superintendent of the hospital. I was informed that the two empty wards were to be taken over by Epsom & Ewell Council and were to be upgraded and converted into accommodation for single parents with children.

This seemed bizarre to me as to coalesce young children adjacent to a 75-bedded long-stay mental health unit could potentially lead to difficulties. The patients at Horton were not in any way dangerous, but some had disinhibited behaviour traits that could be easily misinterpreted as potentially violent, such as responding to voices as a result of hallucinations.

By this time, across the UK it had become increasingly apparent that the brave new world of *Care in the community* was really beginning to struggle. As described in chapter 22. The on-going failures to properly supervise patients in community settings thus resulting in homicides or examples of neglect had not abated.

Increasingly, families were complaining that patients had to break down before they could be admitted to hospital and patients themselves were subject to pressure from the public who were fearful that these people might be dangerous. As a result, the stigma against mental illness and the misgivings about the care of people in the community was rising and there was increasing discomfort on the part of politicians on how to stem these incidents.

It was also at this time that the phenomena of out-of-area placements (OOA's) were rapidly rising. OOA's emerged in the 90's because of a shortfall in bed provision and it was commonplace that patients who were in a crisis being placed in any available mental health unit irrespective of the distance involved. Examples of people being admitted to hospitals hundreds of miles away from where they lived were commonplace. How ironical that the thrust of *Care in the community* was predicated on bringing people back closer to their homes, whereas the reality was that people were being placed distances far away from where they lived.

The organisation *Grant Thorton* in January 2024 reported between May 2022 and April 2023 that there were 4,235 people classified as OOAs. The Government had set itself a target to eradicate OOA's by April 2021 a target they missed.

Some of the examples are perplexing to say the least. For example in 2016, 154 people suffering from eating disorders in England had to go to Scotland, as there were no beds available in England. An eating disorder is one of the most serious of all mental illnesses. Those suffering from the condition have the highest death rate of all psychiatric conditions. The majority of those who suffer from an eating disorder are young women, many in their teens. To become disconnected from your family who may have to travel hundreds of miles to visit you is hardly therapeutic and in many respects seriously adds to the complexity of the condition.

In Devon there were 550 OOA's in the year up to August 2020. Often when people are transferred they become 'lost' in the system. Hard pressed clinicians and managers struggling to cope with the day-to-day pressures move on once someone is safely ensconced elsewhere, the focus switches to the next patient. Furthermore, as result of the low bed provision across the country there is then the on going challenge of discharging patients or transferring people back to near where they live. It is not unknown that people have been left for years in mental health units hundreds of miles from where they live for several years.

The bed provision across the England alone fell from 67,100 in 1987 to 18,400 in 2019, a 73% reduction. Meanwhile corresponding investment in community-based services has not been prioritised. The late 1980's into the 90's covers the intense period of the Hospital closure programme.

In Scotland in July 2019 a highly respected GP, Dr John Budd, blasted the state of Scotland's mental health service as scandalous. Dr Budd said that he regularly found it impossible to get a bed for a mental health patient anywhere in Scotland. He is quoted as saying "We cannot get them into hospital when they need to be in hospital. The only time we can admit people is if they are a direct risk to themselves or others"

How ironical that Scotland can accommodate people from England who suffer from an eating disorder yet do not have adequate provision for general adult mental health beds.

Across the four countries of the UK, acute admission wards are regularly full to capacity and frequently there are patients who are ready for the step down into rehabilitation facilities but due to the shortfall in rehab beds they are stuck. This is bad for their recovery and further compounds the pressure on beds for those requiring admission, which in turn means that those who need help are left until there is a crisis. As a result, there are serious incidents in the community that could have been avoided.

I saw this situation emerging 25 years ago in 1999 and therefore saw an opportunity to develop Horton Haven into a rehabilitation service for people requiring long-term rehab care.

We decided that the decision to house upwards of 30 single parents and their children adjacent to Horton was ill conceived and we put a proposal to Epsom and Ewell district Council that the two empty wards remain in the ownership of the NHS and that we in turn would give them the land on the edge of the campus where the old medical superintendent's house was for the Council to develop the much-needed facility for single parents.

The managers of the Horton Haven at that time were two very capable women, Sheila Gallagher and Madeline Marjoram. These two spent a huge amount of time and effort negotiating the deal, which was eventually resolved in 2006.

In parallel with this I had a number of significant battles to front in relation to this.

The Chair of my own Trust felt that the Horton model was out-of-date and there would not be the need for this type of service. He was also keen to sell the site as he saw the opportunity to bring in a significant capital receipt by selling off the four acres at Horton. He was supported at that time by a senior person at the then London Health Authority who made a powerful case for continuing the rundown and eventual closure of Horton.

In my many encounters with these two, they simply failed to grasp the seriousness of the situation and were very much in the mind set similar to that of the anti-psychiatry movement and MIND that services such as those at Horton were unnecessary.

I will not dilate further on these discussions other than to say I eventually won the day. I had silenced if not converted, my then Chairman and the London Health Authority manager.

In parallel with this Sheila and Madeline successfully concluded the negotiations with the Council and the Trust then invested in converting the two empty wards into high quality residential units. The remainder of the site was also upgraded. Although I had left the Trust in 2007, when the new unit was officially opened, I was invited back and as the then Chair of the Trust, Dame Ruth Runciman and my successor as CEO, Claire Murdoch said in their respective speeches my foresight in retaining the Horton site had put the Trust in a strong position to cope with the undoubted need to provide patients who needed it, with long-term rehabilitation.

Some years later myself and Marjorie Wallace, CEO of the organisation SANE, visited Horton and I was immensely proud of the progress and the valuable contribution this service was making. Marjorie Wallace has been tireless in campaigning to highlight the deficiencies in care that has resulted in untold misery for both those suffering from mental illness and their relatives, quite aside from innocent members of the public who may have been assaulted or even killed by people in a disturbed state who have been failed by the system.

The NHS continues to struggle with OOA's. Had Horton been replicated elsewhere, some of the current pressures in the NHS would have been significantly ameliorated.

There is a touching sequel to the Horton Story.

Many years after the main hospital closed and Horton Haven was up and running there was a poignant event that in many ways bridges the decades and illustrates many of the issues that I have been discussing in this book.

THIS IS THE STORY OF MISS F.

Miss F was born in 1926 and attended school in the London area. It was commonplace for people upon leaving school to enter domestic service where they would live with a family, often for many years. It is known that as a young woman Miss F entered employment with a family to carry out domestic duties and was to do this for some years. However, whist working for the family Miss F became pregnant by her employer, which led to her losing her position and her home. Sadly, when the baby was born, she had to give her daughter up for adoption.

It was not uncommon for unmarried homeless mothers to be admitted to mental hospitals following the birth of their child, generally in order that they might may live in a supported environment usually located out of the inner city and in the countryside. They were often termed 'moral degenerates'.

Miss F was known to have a 'nervous disposition' and mild learning difficulties. She was admitted to Banstead Mental Hospital in Epsom where she lived until Banstead closed in 1986 and she was transferred to Horton.

Her case notes reveal that over the years from her admission Miss F settled into hospital life with little life-changing or major events and the transfer to Horton was uneventful until one day the consultant psychiatrist in charge of her care received a phone call from a woman who claimed to be the daughter of Miss F.

The consultant was informed that this woman who now had a family of her own had attempted many times to trace her mother using traditional methods of searching paper records for information. The family helped in the research and with the growing use of the Internet, searching became easier and quicker. The daughter of this woman (Miss F's granddaughter) had drawn up a list of names the same as Miss F and they set about contacting everyone who shared this. It became apparent with the confirmation of specific details, that Miss F was indeed the mother of the woman conducting the search. Miss F had been in hospital 56 years. Sheila the manager of Horton broke the news to her which was quite an emotional event. She had often thought about what might have become of her baby that was taken from her at birth but had never really discussed it with the staff.

Over the following weeks, Miss F came to terms with the news that her family (that she had no idea existed) had tracked her down and was keen to meet up. The first meeting was carefully planned and took place once Miss F and her daughter were both ready to come together following the long separation that had ensued.

Arrangements were made for the reunion to take place in a coffee shop in the local town and for the reunited mother and daughter it was an emotional and highly successful first meeting. Sheila accompanied Miss F, who describes the meeting as one with lots of tears.

At one point the daughter of Miss F introduced her mother to the waitress stating, "This is my mother. I've never met her before"

Thankfully the relationship with Miss F and her family thrived until the death of Miss F three years later. During this time she enjoyed weekends with her family and was able to join in gatherings such as Christmas and summer barbeques.

This saga encapsulates the injustice and the suffering well into the 20th century of people who were not mentally ill but were victims of hypocrisy. Depositing people into a mental hospital was a convenient way of disposing of an embarrassment. How shocking in a so-called developed mid-20th century country at the time Miss F was incarcerated.

Just pause to think of the fear and the terror she must have felt as a young woman locked away whilst at the same time deprived of her child. It truly is a heart wrenching account and I felt it was important to record this as a reminder of a dark period in the history of our country.

Chapter 22: Care in the Community

The policy colloquially known as 'Care in the Community' overall was a good one.

The basic principle was to provide care for those needing admission closer to home underpinned by a whole host of services to care for people safely in the community. These teams have a myriad of names. *Community mental health teams, early intervention service, assertive outreach, crisis intervention* to mention but a few. The philosophy is to have a menu of services that enabled patients to have quick access to those needing help and when necessary local residential units for those needing admission.

The reality is quite the opposite.

The closure of mental hospital beds has been immense. The figure I referred to earlier of a 75% loss of beds was for England only. In 1955 across the whole of the United Kingdom there were 155,000 beds. By 2018 this had fallen to 23,000 a loss of 132,000 beds.

The UK has a much lower bed provision that comparable countries.

Germany has 120 beds and France 98 beds per 100,000 of population. Whereas the UK has 42 beds per 100k of population.

One of the leading exponents of caring for people in the community is the distinguished psychiatrist Professor Peter Tyrer whom I have had the pleasure of working with. Peter has been at the forefront of maintaining patients' safely in the community. However, he is adamant that to have successful community services they must be underpinned by an adequate provision of inpatient beds. In January 2017 Peter and colleagues in a paper in *The Lancet* described the shortfall in psychiatric beds as an 'Orwellian crisis' I quote from the paper

"Four legs good to legs bad" bleat the sheep in unison in George Orwell's Animal Farm to drown out intelligent criticism whenever raised. "Community good, hospital bad" has been a similar ideological mantra for the past 60 years in psychiatric services. It was appropriate when we had bulging mental hospital in which many patients were merely warehoused, but it has gone too far. We have forgotten the hospital component of community health service, even though it is essential to good practice. While much has been made of innovations in community and extramural care, most observers have barely noticed the steady reduction in bed numbers, particularly in the UK

CONSEQUENCES

Whilst the late 1960's into the 1970's were the era of mental hospital inquires in which whole institutions were investigated, the 1990's was the era of inquiries into the failures of the colloquially known *care in the community*. Throughout the 1990's there were endless inquires into homicides committed by mentally ill people or their suicides. The evidence was overwhelming that the statutory services were unable to cope in the post mental hospital era. Far too often, individual clinicians were held to account and felt demonised, whereas in reality they were being asked at times to do a virtually impossible job.

CHRISTOPHER CLUNIS AND JONATHAN ZITO

In December 1992, newly-wed Jonathan Zito and his wife accompanied by his brother Christopher went to Gatwick airport to meet his parents who were flying in from New York to have a family Christmas. By the time the luggage was loaded into the car, there was not enough room for all five of them so the two brothers took the train back to London. Whilst waiting for a connection at Finsbury Park station, a man whose name was Christopher Clunis wandered onto the platform. Clunis was over 6ft tall and weighed over 18 stone. Several passengers became alarmed by his appearance, which was erratic and bizarre. Christopher Zito beckoned to his brother to move but before he could Clunis attacked him from behind pulling him around and stabbing him in the eye with the knife entering Jonathan's brain.

Clunis then calmly stepped on the waiting train and sat down. Witnesses said he showed no concern or remorse. Two hours later Jonathan Zito died in the Whittington hospital.

What followed was a high-profile inquiry into the care of Christopher Clunis. The inquiry revealed a fragmented service with multiple agencies involved. The report of the Clunis case is a litany of poor communication, buck passing and a mental health service unable to cope with a person with longstanding schizophrenia and a history of violence. Just eight days before he killed Jonathan Zito, he had attacked a man with a screwdriver in London and later that day he terrified a group of women and children brandishing a screwdriver.

He had copious admissions to different psychiatric units. There was no continuity of care and every service, the NHS, Social Services, the police, probation service all came in for criticism.

Whilst Jonathan Zito was a victim so was Clunis.

The Clunis inquiry is a seminal point of time in mental health policy and practice across the UK. The public and politicians were shocked that in a developed country a man of Christopher Clunis's disposition could not be properly cared for and kept safe for his own sake let alone that of the public. He was severely ill and to all intents 'insane' yet the services were unable to help him and the young life of Jonathan Zito was needlessly wasted.

Had it not been for the tenacity of his wife, Jayne the full extent of the catastrophic failures of Clunis's care may not have been fully realised.

For many years Jayne headed up the Jonathan Zito Trust pushed for reform and was successful in keeping the failures of the system in the public arena. The Zito Trust ran from 1994 to 2009. It achieved many of its objectives including the establishment of Community Treatment Orders. Since Jonathan Zito's death there have been 400 official inquiries into homicides by people with mental illness. This has cost countless millions however a cursory examination of their findings reveals that any recommendations that has financial implications are rarely implemented and it is common of the organisations who may be criticised to say 'We intend to learn from this tragic event". The evidence would suggest this is not the case.

Inquires are still held but they do not attract the same level of publicity presumably because nothing new is being said. It's as though these acts have become 'normalised 'which is a sad indictment.

Chapter 23: Inspectorates and regulators

Over the years there have been a number of initiatives to monitor and regulate mental hospitals. From 1913 to 1959 the Board of Control were tasked with inspecting the hospitals. It's difficult to comment on how effective they were due to a lack of records and I'm sure an acceptance that the regime to keep people contained was the primary objective and as they were successful in that area it was assumed that there was no cause for concern.

HOSPITAL ADVISORY SERVICE (HAS)

The HAS was set up in 1970 following the emerging scandals and concerns initially triggered by the Ely Hospital inquiry.

The HAS consisted of a panel of people who would spend several days visiting a hospital and making recommendations on their observations and findings. It was also tasked with identifying and spreading good practice, which I believe they were quite successful at.

The HAS was really no different to the different iterations of inspectorates there has been over the years. They are like the proverbial curate's egg, good in places.

With the right team and a constructive mentality they were a force for good. When this was not the case they could prove to be very unhelpful to the point of utterly demoralising and damaging to a hospital.

An example that is worth dilating on is one relayed to me by a friend who was working in another hospital.

In this hospital there was a patient who had a genetic disorder and was only was 4′ 5″ tall. In addition, he was a schizophrenic and hypomanic. At night he would not sleep in a bed but had for many years slept in a laundry bag at his insistence in the clinic room adjacent to where the night nurses sat. He was a chain smoker and would pick up discarded cigarettes and constantly ask for a light. Once in the laundry bag he would settle down and would sleep soundly. Over the years many efforts were attempted to try to get him to sleep in a bed all without success. If he was placed in bed he would become distressed and disturbed. At one stage he was put in a side room, which was locked with the objective that he would eventually settle down and sleep in the bed. This too was unsuccessful and he had become very disturbed in the room shouting screaming and banging on the door begging to be allowed to get into the laundry bag to which the staff eventually relented.

His way of sleeping was accepted as a manifestation of

his illness. During an inspection from the HAS his ward received a night visit. After going around the ward the two inspectors went to the clinic room to discuss with the two nurses how things were in the ward. The conversation was perfectly convivial and appeared to be going well. At one point an inspector noticed some movement in the laundry bag that was in the corner of the room. The nurses explained the situation, which left the inspectors incredulous, and they asked that the bag be opened. On doing do so the patient popped up and immediately asked for a light.

The upshot of all of this was that the inspectors the next day were highly critical of the management of the patient and insisted that he be placed in a bed and if need be in a side room until he accepted that he should be sleeping in a conventional way. That night he was locked in a side room and he refused to get in the bed. He eventually became highly distressed, banging on the door he was frightened and pleading with the staff to let him out, begging for his laundry bag. This went on for several hours and eventfully the nurses let him revert to is preferred way of sleeping. The HAS were highly critical and reported this in their report of their inspection of the hospital. The consultant psychiatrist responsible for the patient supported the nurses, unlike the senior management, who felt that there should be a solution, however, they were unable to offer anything constructive.

This type of example encapsulates how at times inspectorates can be so detached from the reality of complex clinical challenges that are often resolved/managed in an unconventional way but might be in the patient's best interests.

THE MENTAL HEALTH ACT COMMISSION (MHAC)

The Mental Health Act Commission was established by an Act of Parliament in 1983.

Its remit is to ensure that people who are detained under the Act are done so in accordance with the Act's legal requirements. There are only two situations when a citizen of the UK can be lose their liberty without going through the criminal justice courts, one is under public health legislation the other is the Mental Health Act. It is vital therefore that the legal and human rights of individuals are safeguarded. The importance of correct assessment combined with the right of appeal is paramount. The Commission also has visiting rights and are tasked to provide an annual report to the Secretary of State of Health. As discussed with the HAS in the previous chapter the Commission can be a force for good but also at times can be unintentionally unhelpful. It's now over 40 years since their inception and overall, the Commission has done much to ensure compliance with the Act and has become a vehicle for identifying deficiencies in care, addressing poor standards and attitudes. They have also become an agent for identifying good practice. The Commission has a monitoring role as opposed to an inspectorate or that of a regulator.

As with all organisations it's the leadership from the top that determines the effectiveness of the organisation. Between1994 and 1998 under the stewardship of one of its Chairs, Dame Ruth Runciman, the Commission developed into a highly dynamic and effective organisation that did much to help maintain and raise standards of care. During her tenure as Chair of the Commission she rigorously tightened up the application of the requirements of the Act, ensuring that patients were legally detained. Although this may seem obvious, the reality was that hitherto there were frequent problems identified with the administration of the Act. Incomplete paperwork and examples of patients not being fully informed on how to appeal against detention were not uncommon. There were often poor arrangements when holding appeals against detention and copious examples of key people such as the approved social workers being ill prepared or responsible medical officers either not appearing on time or not at all to hearings.

Among the many initiatives and developments in Dame Ruth's era was the concept of un-announced visits. I well remember one Saturday evening when dozens of mental health units in different parts of the country had unannounced visits commencing at 10pm. This in my view was an entirely legitimate and desirable thing to do. The 24-hour nature of care is such that it's important that the service should be operating to the highest standards at all times. The Commission was an essential component in helping to monitor services.

Despite my respect for many of the people that I have worked with from the MHAC there are two examples when I was CEO of the Central and North West London NHS trust where I had a direct clash with the MHAC.

The first concerned an incident on a Christmas Eve. I received a call from the consultant psychiatrist responsible for one of our locked wards saying that he had received a phone call from Paddington Green police station that they had a 15-year-old girl in custody who was acutely mentally ill and there was not an adolescent bed across London to be found for her. This girl had arrived at Paddington station and her home was several hundred miles from London. At a loss to find a bed the consultant had been asked if it was possible to admit her to an adult ward. I met with the consultant, and we decided that on balance it would be better to admit this child to an adult ward and to keep her constantly chaperoned by a female nurse rather than leave her in a police cell over Christmas and possibly into the New Year.

In accordance with the required protocol that every time a minor is admitted to an adult ward the Mental Health Act Commission should be informed, I telephoned them. This was 12 mid-day and there was a message on their phone saying that they were now closed until after the New Year. I left a message on the phone and also emailed them giving full details, stressing that this was an humanitarian act and that in my opinion to admit was the best option from a poor hand. Better to be in a ward with the ability to take exercise and be properly supervised rather than alone in a cell. The girl actually did well in the ward and a few days into January an adolescent bed was located back near her home and she was duly transferred.

On the first day back after the holiday I received a call from a senior manager at the MHAC who was high handed, officious and superior in tone. He demanded to know what I was thinking of, admitting a child to an adult ward and going on to say that the Commission would be making a highly critical report of the Trust's actions. I responded by giving this person a piece of my mind, later described by one of my colleagues who was with me as 'Giving them both barrels" As a result there was an instant climb down and the critical report never appeared. I also put it to this person that what they should be doing is bringing to the attention of senior civil servants and the Secretary of State's office just how unsatisfactory it is that in a country such as the UK there was not a single bed available for a child over Christmas and New Year. This type of intervention was not uncommon and only sought to create tensions between those providing services and the Commission. It demonstrates how at times people in these positions can be detached from the reality of providing services with less than adequate resources. Being criticised is not really going to help address these deficits.

The second example concerns the locked unit at the Park Royal Centre for Mental Health. The catchment area that the CNWL Trust serves has a high density of people from the Black and Asian communities. In the London borough of Brent the term 'Ethnic minority" is a misnomer. The majority of the people are black. Within the mental health complex at the Park Royal Centre for Mental Health we had an 18-bedded locked unit that cared for men who had significantly disturbed and challenging behaviour. At any time the majority of the patients in this unit were black.

The MHAC carried out a visit to this unit and expressed concern that of the 18 patients 16 were black. During their discussions with the staff a theme emerged that suggested the service was institutionally racist. The local manager and the consultant telephoned me to express their concern. They were both highly disconcerted at the prospect of being labelled racist. This in turn would be damaging to staff morale and would be reflect badly on the unit with families and stakeholders. In addition, the local media who would become aware of the report and understandably would cover the story.

I decided to go to the unit to meet with the commissioners. My colleagues and I explained in our meeting with the Commission that in a borough such as Brent most of the patients would be black because that represents the population we serve. The meeting became very difficult and we were subjected to comments such as 'culturally insensitive' and 'institutionally racist'. Frequent mention was made to the fact that black people are four times more likely to be detained under the Mental Heath Act than white people.

I was at pains to point out that were acutely aware of this but to put the responsibility for this at the door of the mental health service was misplaced. I gave these people what amounted to a tutorial of the causation of mental illness. I mentioned poverty, socio economic deprivation, poor housing, lack of job opportunities, drugs and alcohol, racism and social isolation.

Of the 16 black men who were detained on the unit 5 had cannabis induced psychosis. The others had a combination of seriously disturbed behaviour as result of schizophrenia, bi-polar disorder and/or alcohol and other addictive drugs. I further put it to the Commissioners that if they were so sure that we were admitting patients inappropriately then they had the power to discharge them. I pointed to the cabinet that contained the patients' case notes and suggested that the go through them and decide who they should release. I also said that if they chose to disregard what I was putting to them and if we received a critical report alleging racism then I would challenge it. I had no intention of doing what often happens that those running organisations accept the criticism and make statements such as "We can learn from this" right through to making statements along the lines of having to accept there are racist practices. I hasten to add that of course I know there are racists in British society and there are examples of services that are culturally insensitive but, in my experience, psychiatrists are among the most liberal minded people you could wish to meet and far from being culturally insensitive I believe most of them work hard to try to relate to the cultural needs of their patients. My challenge to the commission to discharge patients was not taken up.

I referred to the work of Professors Swaran Singh from Warwick and Robin Murray of the Institute of Psychiatry.

Both have studied the issue of racism and mental illness and that I expected the commission to be familiar with their work. It was apparent they were not.

One of the other worrying aspects of these types of ill-informed appraisal of services is that it further reinforces the distrust of the mental health services within the black community. This in turn often leads to late presentations for help, as those in need of help are reluctant to seek it due to the poor publicity the mental health services frequently receive. Whenever I discuss or write about this particular issue I am at pains to point out that the vast majority of black people will never have the need to seek psychiatric help. There is a danger that the impression is given that black people have a higher preponderance to become mentally ill. The evidence is clear, this is not the case.

Until we have a discourse over the causation of mental illness and the bespoke needs of people from different ethnicities the current difficulties will continue. We know there is a need to develop culturally aware services, and to ensure there is trust from all ethnic backgrounds, to ensure early access to services.

Chapter 24: The issues facing mental health in the 2020's.

Mental health services were under strain before the pandemic, and this has been exacerbated because of it.

Claire Murdoch as National Director for Mental Health is working hard to address many of the issues I have mentioned.

For Claire's efforts to be successful there will have to be a fundamental change in the mind set in relation to bed provision. In addition, the NHS will need more financial resources to fund what is still in effect a Cinderella service. There is much talk about 'Parity of esteem' and phrases such as 'No health without mental health' roll easily off the tongue. These phrases will become 'hymns to virtue' unless they are supported with the resources and policies that are needed. There has been an increase in financial investment into mental health services, but more does not equate too enough. Furthermore, this is on the back of decades of underinvestment.

WHERE WE ARE IN 2024

I feel the need to summarise my thoughts to ensure there is no misunderstanding as to my views.

In relation to the mental hospitals. In the 1960's, because of better clinical interventions, combined with a wider range of drug therapies, the number of people in hospital had declined. Consequently, there were too many hospitals and there were still people who did not need to be in hospital and could have been cared for in the community with the right support.

Some mental hospitals were very well managed, others not so.

Rather than wholesale closure there should have been a significant reduction in the size but a recognition that there would be a need for a decent bed stock to not only help those who are acutely ill but for those who need longer term residential care.

The undoubted advances in psychiatry have been immense since the emergence of Largactil in the 1950's. This is not only in relation to a wide range of highly effective drugs but the development of roles such as community psychiatric nurses and a whole of host of other disciplines that either obviate the need for admission or after discharge, can help people to live normal lives whilst being maintained in the community.

The evidence is compelling that aspects of mental health policy has failed.

The countless inquires into the homicide and suicides with the recurring themes of under resourced and fragmented services continue unabated. Far too often there is a failure to fully implement the recommendations of these inquires. I have said in conferences on mental health policy that a critique of the inquiry findings would reveal that in far too many examples, the recommendations that are implemented are those that do not have any resource implications.

PRISONERS

The prison population is inflated with people who should be receiving treatment in a mental health unit rather than prisons.

In 2017 a Westminster Parliament report by the Committee of Public Accounts in its report: *Mental Health in Prisons* stated:

The current system of self-inflicted deaths and self-harm incidents in prisons is appalling and the system for improving the mental health of prisoners isn't working, as it should. The

Government does not have reliable or up to date measures of the number of prisoners who have mental health problems and the existing screening procedures are insufficient to adequately identify those who need support and treatment.

This is compelling evidence by MP's that the prison system is not the place for people who are mentally ill. Most prisons now have psychiatric wings and many struggle to provide the level of service needed. Prisoners are nearly four times more likely to die by suicide than the general population and in a damming report by the prisons ombudsman it was reported that in 2018 there was a 23% rise in suicides.

HOMELESSNESS

Public Health England estimates that 50% of people who sleep rough have mental health problems. When I was CEO of CNWL NHS Trust we had a team that worked on the streets of Westminster caring and supporting those with mental health problems. On a number of occasions, I worked a night shift with the team. What was abundantly clear was that the need in relation to rough sleepers was huge, and I suspect in many other parts of the country this need is unmet.

ACUTE ADMISSION WARDS

I'm saddened to say that many of the acute admission wards are not therapeutic environments that are conducive to good recovery. They are frequently overcrowded and have an inappropriate mix of patients.

In February 2024 Rebecca Thomas of the *The Independent* newspaper reported that following an in-depth inquiry, that over the previous five years almost 20,000 reports of sexual incidents on psychiatric wards have been made. Dr Lade Smith president of the Royal College of Psychiatrists called the findings "horrendous".

Among the key revelations were:

- At least 19,899 sexual incidents were reported across more that 30 NHS trusts between 2019 and 2023, including staff assaults on patients and patients assaulting each other.
- The figures suggest that just 982, less than 5 percent of sexual incidents were reported to the police over the same period.
- 800 allegations of rape and serious assaults on women.
- Mixed sex wards, despite being banned a decade ago, are still in use across NHS mental health care with more than 500 reports of sexual assault since 2019.

- Just six out of 50 hospitals were able to prove they were meeting NHS standards aimed at protecting patients from sexual harm.

Some patients are often ready for transfer to other units but cannot be transferred because of the lack of move on facilities. There are examples of people being kept in hospital for years for the want of appropriate move on places. In addition, most people admitted to acute admission wards are now on detention orders as admission is frequently delayed until there is a crisis. This in turn leads to longer lengths of stay.

Chapter 25: Winterbourne View and Whorlton Hall.

In the summer of 2019, I met up with a long-time friend, Bob Andrews, we trained as psychiatric nurses at the same hospital. Bobby left nursing shortly after qualifying and went on to have a successful career as a businessman. Among his many enterprises he started the live music scene at the *Horn of Plenty* pub in St Albans. For those who are not aware, this venue became a launch pad for several high-profile singers and bands and is still to this day one of the places to play.

Nowadays he lives in Florida and we met on one of his visits back to the UK.

At our meeting we eventually got around to discussing our experiences from all those years ago when we were students together. A few months earlier there was the exposé by the BBC of the shocking cruelty at Whorlton Hall the unit in Durham that cared for people with autism and learning difficulties. The level of abuse and cruelty the undercover film revealed, included the deliberate provocation of residents. Mental cruelty and threats to patients were the norm. With one particular woman who had a phobia about men, two male members of staff taunted her by saying that her room would be inundated with men. This caused her huge distress and the two members of staff are caught on film laughing and enjoying the distress.

The Whorlton Hall documentary came 8 years after another exposé of the care home Winterbourne View near Bristol for people with learning difficulties and challenging behaviour where there were shocking examples of abject cruelty also revealed by undercover filming by a BBC reporter. There were examples of staff kicking and thumping people. Others of stamping on the hands of residents. A staff member, Wayne Rogers, is filmed having placed a chair over a young woman trapping her. She is in distress and another member of staff covers her face with a blanket. It is cruelty and abuse of staggering levels all in front of other staff members and of course other residents. As a result there was a police investigation and six members of staff were imprisoned including the ringleader, Wayne Rogers, who was sentenced to two years. Five others members of staff were given suspended prison sentences. The two registered nurses who were also guilty were struck off the Nursing Council register.

Both films shocked the nation. The regulator, the CQC had to acknowledge that despite their inspections they had not detected the abuse.

Bobby and I discussed how that type of gratuitous abuse would not have been tolerated in the hospital where we trained. In fact, the opposite was the case. The whole approach in the old mental hospitals was on containment and doing everything to ensure that patients did not become upset or agitated. I hasten to add at this point that the inquiries into the mental hospitals that I have mentioned did reveal examples of poor treatment and care on the part of some staff but this was the exception. The abuse at Whorlton Hall and Winterbourne View, the two places I have mentioned would not have been tolerated. Both of the facilities had a significant number of unqualified staff and the undercover filming revealed their ability to be able to inflict abuse and suffering the like and level of which Bobby and myself never witnessed in our training and in my case never at different times my career.

The case I referred to earlier involving John and Elizabeth differs from these examples in that this was an individual who behaved appallingly as opposed to the wholesale approach by staff inflicting cruelty with a sense of impunity. Staff were boasting about how they abused people. I'm appalled that at Winterbourne View there were registered nurses who were indifferent to the attitude of the care assistants.

The regime in mental hospitals was as I have said was

one of containment. The term "know your patients" was frequently used. This meant knowing what did or did not agitate or upset patients. For example, the patient I mentioned who thought he was a chair, would sit for hours quietly observing the world around him. He sat in the same part of the ward every day and was allowed to sit there in peace. It was well known that if anyone decided to suggest to him that he was not a chair or if someone sat in his place he would become very aggressive. Therefor both staff and his fellow patients were aware of this and left him to his own devices.

When I reflect on the standard of the ward sisters and charge nurses that I worked with they would have not permitted the outrage revealed in the two examples I have referred to. I can visualise them reproaching people asking what on earth did they think they were doing by deliberate creating problems when what we wish, is to get through day with minimal problems.

57 years on from the Ely Hospital inquiry how depressing, currently, when the old "closed institutions" have closed after coming in for so much criticism that such unbridled cruelty could occur. The countless policy initiatives, the high level of expenditure on inspectorates, the sentiments such as "No health without mental health" and "Parity of esteem" all seem so pointless.

The fallout from the Winterbourne View scandal resulted in the development of the policy *Transforming Care.*

The basic principles of this policy are sound. Every effort should be made to prevent unnecessary admission to hospital and to promote as independent living for people with learning difficulties as possible.

Targets were set to reduce the number of people in hospital. The problem was that the targets were far too ambitious and as with the failures in mental health policy, there was a lack of recognition of the complexity of the challenges some people with a learning difficulty or conditions such as autism face.

The targets were lowered but were still not being met.

In January 2020 Mencap published a report stating that the Government and the NHS are at risk of missing their targets. The ideology of independent living is flawed. Some people with learning difficulties or autism simply cannot cope living alone. Placing them in flats where all they have is visits from paid carers is not good. Much better for these people to be living with others where they can enjoy friendship and companionship. Small residences of four to six people seems ideal to me.

In February 2021 it was revealed that the target that had been revised down to be met in 2019, had not been achieved and it has now been extended to 2024.

Transforming Care is in danger of mirroring the mistakes made with mental health policy which presupposes that staffed residential care is either unneeded or you do not need as much of it.

Wrong, we need to ensure there is a mixed economy of provision that can help those with severe learning difficulties and autism with challenging behaviour, across the spectrum to those who may have a learning difficulty and autism but can live independently. I predict that if the current policy is not checked then in time there will be further scandals of people being found neglected and isolated, living alone with unfulfilling lives.

In any other walk of life if you keep missing a target or objective it would be re-visited not simply extended. Meanwhile managers are being judged on a failure to implement a policy that is flawed but it is resulting in pressure to keep placing people into accommodation that is not appropriate for their needs.

Chapter 26: Staffing and a poorly managed service

STAFFING

Both mental health and learning difficulty nursing have suffered from huge cut backs over many years. Between 2009 and 2019 there was 10.6% loss of the number of mental health nurses, 6,000 in total. In the same ten years there was a marked increase in work and referrals. Similarly there was a loss of 2,309 learning disability nursing posts between 2009 and 2019. This is a sad indictment of the value placed on having properly trained nurses and does not bode well for the future.

A POORLY MANAGED SERVICE

By 2006 I had been the CEO of the Central & North West London NHS Trust for nearly 12 years. I loved my time at CNWL. The Trust enjoyed a huge amount of respect. We had won a number of awards and I had led the Trust up to Secretary of State's approval for Foundation Trust status. As well as performing well on a wide range of clinical indicators we also had very strong financial management and for 12 consecutive years we balanced our books and met all of our financial targets. By maintaining a tight grip on the finances meant we were able to use any new money to develop services and to avoid having to cut back on badly needed clinical services to stay in financial balance.

In 2006 I received a phone call from the CEO of the Northwest London Strategic Health Authority. It was explained to me that the mental health services in an NHS Trust also in London had collapsed. He outlined the problems which were a combination of poor management resulting in a significant financial deficit plus a wide range of other issues that were giving serious cause for concern and he wished CNWL to take over running these services.

This was a phone call that on one hand I will not deny is very flattering, but on the other hand gives serious pause for thought. Taking on a failing service is not without its challenges and can suck in a lot of time.

Accordingly, we decided for myself and a member of my team to meet with the senior manager of the service. On arriving at the management offices, which were also located on the main site for the inpatient, psychiatric unit we were pleasantly surprised because the unit was a relatively new build and was pleasing in appearance. However, when we arrived at the main entrance, we noticed that one of the doors was boarded up with plywood. It was also apparent that this plywood had been there for sometime as the wood was weatherworn and had a significant amount of graffiti on it.

We met with the manager who I knew from the past and the meeting went reasonably well. The manager was somewhat nervous and quite understandably wanted to give their account as to why things were not in good shape. We heard about a myriad of difficulties. At the end of a long meeting and after working through many of the issues I mentioned the door of the unit and was informed that a patient had kicked the panel in some months ago. I was told that there was no money in the maintenance budget to repair it. The significance of why I draw attention to this I will explain later.

Over the next few weeks we then had meetings with social services, MP's, carers and patients to talk through the issues and the implications of coming under the auspices of another NHS Trust. We also held meetings with the trade unions and of course with the staff.

Accordingly, the transfer of service went ahead. In the course of gathering information we were informed of a number of serious and worrying issues. One of which was that a consultant psychiatrist had been under suspension on full pay for four years. We were told that there had been a conflict within the team in which this doctor worked and that grievances had been lodged. Things had reached an impasse between the psychiatrist and the staff involved, and the local management had been unable to resolve the issues.

The costs were staggering. The psychiatrist was on a salary of £100k pa and the locum and agency Doctors to cover his absence were £200k PA. In total therefore the cost was well over a million pounds over four years. In addition, there were substantial legal fees and yet still no resolution. Within a relatively short space of time we resolved the matter and brought the saga to an end. Although it's many years ago I will not dilate on the solution as a compromise agreement was signed and it would not be appropriate. I am however satisfied that our solution was the correct one and that the whole issue should have never got so out of hand. It was indefensible that this went on for four years and that the managers did not have any idea how to resolve it. I have occasionally reflected how long it would have gone on had we not intervened

As part of my management style I always liked to spend time visiting wards and departments. It's the best way to get a feel for service. I have worked in situations where too much reliance is placed on reading papers at Board meetings as a way of understanding the services whereas in my experience you need to do both.

Shortly after taking over I decided to visit some of the wards. I remember my first visit so well. It was a Friday afternoon at about 4pm. I had just finished a meeting with some of the staff at the unit and decided to go "Walk about"

I went to one of the acute admission wards and found the door locked. This is not unusual in this day and age as nowadays most people who are inpatients are on detention orders. I rang the ward bell and looked through the glass panel and could see that down the end of a long passage where there were a group of people. I assumed that some of the people were staff and others patients. These people were milling around and eventually I rang the bell again with still no reaction. I then rang it a third time, which resulted in a man ambling down the passage towards the door. He was slovenly dressed and looked disinterested. On unlocking the door he opened it just a few Inches and said "What?"

I in turn replied, "What do you mean, what"

His reply, 'What do you want"

"I want to come in"

"Who are you"?

"I'm your new Chief Executive".

"Oh, sorry I didn't realise who you were"

With that the man stood aside and let me in. I asked who he was and he explained he was a member of the nursing staff. I asked him who was in charge of the ward. He replied and said that the ward manager was in his office and I asked him to show me to the office. As we walked along he said again that he was sorry, as he didn't recognise me. When we arrived at the office I asked him to come in with me.

The ward manager recognised me as he been in some of the staff meetings. I explained my encounter with his member of staff who for about the fourth time said that he didn't recognise me. I then put it to him that I was the least of his worries. I could have been someone's brother, father, friend, employer visiting the unit and I did not expect to be greeted with a "What' I said that I found his whole attitude unacceptable let alone his dishevelled appearance. I went to say that when I'm in a supermarket looking for a product the store assistants do not greet my inquiry with "what" In fact quite the opposite and I made the point that I get more respect and better customer service in a supermarket than I received from this nurse. I also said if that was his attitude to me I dread to think about his attitude to patients.

He looked suitably chastised and I asked him to leave the

office. The charge nurse immediately said that he was so pleased that I had reproached the man and went on to say that his attitude was appalling. I replied that I was concerned that as the charge nurse of the ward he had not done anything about it. In response he said that if he had tried, he was doubtful if he would get any support from his managers. He said that they rarely saw managers and that past experience had led him to reach the conclusion that there was no point in trying to do something about people like this man due to his ineffective superiors.

In view of what I had gleaned already about the service we had taken over I had some sympathy with him.

The following Tuesday I had a prearranged open meeting with all staff. There was a large attendance upwards of 100 staff. In this meeting I spoke only about my concerns about the service and that we needed to have a fundamental reappraisal as to how we were going to go forward and turn things around. I gave a detailed account of my encounter with the nurse the previous Friday afternoon even though the man was at the meeting. I did not single him out, as that would have been unnecessary but I was not backwards in using it as an example of just how poor the standards were in some areas. I was careful to make the point that I knew there would be plenty of examples of good work and that from my experience most people would be trying to do a good job.

And so, we set about systematically addressing the many issues that needed addressing. We brought in new managers and fundamentally changed the dynamic. The rate of progress was quick and as always in my experience once staff have good local leadership they respond positively.

A few months after our takeover I was visiting the services and a senior member of one of the allied health professions stopped me on a corridor and said how happy both her and her colleagues were with the way things had changed. She then proceeded to say that it was particularly impressive how we addressed the issue of the consultant who had been suspended for several years. I immediately stopped her and said that it was inappropriate to discuss that subject with me. Her reply was along the lines of 'Oh yes of course but we all know what occurred" I was about to reproach her when she went on to ask why hadn't we resolved the other long-term suspension.

It transpired that a senior member of one of the allied health professions, had been on suspension for four years (a coincidence that it was the same period of time as the psychiatrist). Two members of staff had an unpleasant working relationship that deteriorated into open acrimony and both members of staff had lodged grievances against each other. Following an investigation, it was decided that the solution was that the two should be redeployed so that they were not working together. One of the two accepted this, the other did not and refused to be redeployed insisting that she was not at fault. As there was the classic stand off this person was sent on gardening leave and astonishingly four years later was still on full paid leave.

I could hardly believe what I was hearing and so for the second time we had to resolve something that had not only cost the tax payer tens of thousands of pounds but should have been addressed four years earlier. The members of staff should have been given the opportunity to be redeployed and if one refused, disciplinary action should have been instigated.

To further emphasise just how lamentable the management of these services were, is an issue that the person who refused to be redeployed, took up with her managers.

There is a facility in the NHS for people who use their cars for work on a regular basis to receive a financial 'Regular user allowance'. When working, this person used her car for work and was entitled to this allowance. Whilst on suspension the allowance was stopped because she was not using her car for work.

She contested this saying that it was not her fault that she was not working and that she was entitled to the allowance. As a result, it was reinstated. Therefor for four years an entitlement was paid for an expense that was not incurred. Although the sum of money involved pales when compared to the four years of full salary it illustrates just how poor the management were.

I could not help but reflect there was not a budget to fix the broken panel on the front door of the unit but a sum of money well over £1million was spent needlessly on these suspensions.

Mental health services are always under pressure due to lack of funding and this is an example of poor management in the extreme. This is so unfortunate as there are countless examples of high-quality management, but this was an example of the very poorest leadership.

Although this psychiatric unit was in the grounds of a general hospital it was in many respects as isolated as the old institutions. Why did it take the random visit by the new CEO to reveal the appalling attitude of the nurse who so discourteously answered the door to me? Managers should have been walking the job, speaking with patients, visitor's and of course the staff. Clearly was not happening.

Chapter 27: Conclusions

So, as I come to the end of this book, I hope people will understand my motive for writing it.

I thought it would be helpful to restate and clarify my thoughts.

First of all, this book is not a call to re-open the old mental hospitals. Far from it, I have written there were too many of them and some were not well managed.

The care model was out of date and a more progressive and enlightened approach had emerged to care for those who suffer from mental illness. Too many of the staff working in these hospitals failed to move with the times.

What is not the case is that all mental hospitals were uniformly bad. I witnessed at first hand some outstanding care and many people derived help and support from the countless dedicated staff across a wide range of disciplines. Nurses, occupational therapists, art and music therapists, social workers, psychiatrists and psychologists plus many more.

My criticism is of the wholesale closure and a lack of recognition that to provide high quality community-based care this has to be underpinned by a good level of inpatient beds and facilities. As I have demonstrated the

UK has a ratio of beds to population far below that of comparable countries.

I am unreservedly critical of the failure to invest the capital receipts from the disposal of the estates of the mental hospitals into the reprovision. In reality with a few notable exceptions the re-provision was either done on the cheap or were in NHS buildings that were surplus to requirements as demonstrated by the Gordon Hospital example.

Acute admission wards are not therapeutic environments. They are full to capacity and there are examples of patients having to sleep on the floor, as there are no beds available. Some years back at a Mental Health NHS Trust in London this was commonplace and when criticised by the regulator, the response was "It's better than nowhere", what an appalling statement. The Victorians had created a network of Hospitals that ensured patients did not have to sleep on the floor. Progress, I think not.

As well as being full to overflowing there are also additional problems. Due to the shortage of beds psychiatrists frequently have to wait until there is a crisis before they can admit. This usually means via a detention order hence the need to lock the wards. This is then compounded by a lack of step-down beds meaning there are delayed discharges further compounding the problem. People have to stay in locked acute admission wards with highly disturbed patients when what they need is longer-term rehabilitation.

As I have commented earlier, the bed shortage results in '*Out of area placements*' often this means placing patients hundreds of miles from their homes. In the summer of 2019, I was covering the vacant post of Chair at the North Middlesex NHS University Hospital Trust and on one Saturday afternoon there were 12 people who had severe mental health problems in the A&E department and the nearest available bed was in Bristol.

The litany of concerns across mental health services is a matter of huge concern.

As of February 2024, there are several inquiries underway:

1) In Essex there is the *Lampard inquiry* that has been tasked to investigate mental health deaths in inpatient settings between 1st January 2000 and 31st December 2023. It is reported in the press that there could be around 2,000 deaths that this inquiry will cover.

2) The police are investigation concerns raised by relatives of patients under the care of the Norfolk and Suffolk NHS Foundation Trust into

thousands of deaths of mental health patients. A report by the audit firm *Grant Thornton* concluded that the Trust has simply lost track of those who had died. It is reported that between 2019 and 2022 more than 8,000 patients died unexpectantly, and, for three quarters, the Trust did not know how or why, the *Grant Thornton* report found.

3) In Northern Ireland there is an inquiry chaired by Tom Kark KC into abuse at Muckamore Abbey Hospital. There are allegations of abuse and a significant number of staff have been suspended and at least 38 people have been arrested by the police who are carrying out an investigation in parallel to the Kark inquiry.

4) A review has been ordered by Health Secretary Victoria Atkins into the care of Valdo Calocane who fatally stabbed students Barnaby Webber and Grace O'Malley-Kumar before killing caretaker Ian Coates in June 2023. This case attracted widespread publicity and has resulted in significant concern being expressed by the public over their confidence in the mental health care system across the country.

5) A report into the Greater Manchester Mental Health NHS Foundation Trust was published in February 2024 following an undercover investigation by the BBC programme *Panorama.* The programme exposed shocking levels of abuse, humiliation and bullying of patients across the Edenfield Centre in Prestwich. The report concluded that there was a closed culture, including an absence of psychological safety, incivility between staff, poor leadership and a lack of team working.

6) In Scotland an inquiry is underway into the abuse suffered by children in residential care in17 institutions across Scotland including psychiatric hospitals run by the NHS.

It would be wrong to speculate on the outcome of the inquires that have yet to report.

In addition to these high-profile inquiries there are many more that have not attracted the same level of publicity.

There are however some recurring themes. So many of the allegations and concerns emanate from relatives, carers, junior members of staff or from undercover reporters. There is very little evidence that inspectorates such as the CQC or senior managers reveal these shocking events.

I wish those such as Claire Murdoch National Director for Mental Health services and Tim Kendall the former National Director for Clinical Mental Health Services well as they strive to roll back the years of poor planning and under resourcing.

As for me, despite the challenges I feel so lucky to have been introduced to the world of mental health nursing by my old school friend Roger Whybrow. I'm still trying to make my contribution and I keep I touch with many of my colleagues from the different jobs I have had over the years.

My admiration of so many people I have worked with is immeasurable, ranging from those when I commenced in 1968 to the present day.

Most of all my wish is for those who suffer from mental illness to really have the parity of esteem that is spoken about so easily but is hard to deliver. If that could be achieved it would be the step forward we all would wish.

I sometimes find myself driving by the sites of the old mental hospitals. The up-market housing developments have all been tastefully developed around the trees with lots of open space. In some of the developments the wards have been converted into apartments. I see children playing in the grounds and I can't help but wonder if they have any idea of the tales the trees could recant if they could speak. I think of the barbeques that people will be having under the shade of the trees that just few short years ago were in the courtyards of the wards. The contrast could not be greater. I'm frequently in London and I see people who are mentally ill sleeping rough and I know there could have been a better place for them.

Most of the people who planned and executed the demise of the mental hospitals have probably long retired and in their dotage may be trading off their so-called achievements. I wish them no ill will, but I do know they were misguided, however well intended. In many respects the lot of the mentally ill is in fact far worse than what it was when there was an adequate bed stock.

My hope, however forlorn, is that a reappraisal of need is undertaken as *Care in the Community* only works effectively when it is underpinned by an adequate provision of in-patient beds.

I genuinely feel privileged to have worked with people who have mental health problems. The increase in the involvement of patients in the planning and delivery of services has been a very welcome development over the past few years.

I wish all of those either receiving help from the mental health services or those who working with them every strength and support as we face the on-going challenges.

Finally, my thoughts are with the many people I have worked with over the past 50 years and more who came to the UK from overseas. The NHS continues to be one of the headline features in the news, currently because of the effects of the Covid pandemic but even in the non-covid times it is rarely out of the news.

There have been a number of TV documentaries in recent times celebrating the contribution of people who came from the Caribbean to train as nurses from the early 1950's onwards. These people were most welcome and have made an enormous contribution to our health service.

The ethnic group that does not receive the recognition they undoubtedly deserve are the young women and men from Ireland who from the 1940's have been coming to the UK to train and work as nurses. For many years they were the biggest ethnic group other than the indigenous population and I would like to pay tribute to them.

I have found over the years that Irish people have very good 'people' skills and are by nature, naturally empathetic. The Irish education system is such that written and numerical skills are well developed, they are good teachers and have time for students, interspersed with a good sense of humour

Thank you also to the nurses from India, Pakistan, Malaysia, Mauritius, the Philippines, Zimbabwe and many other countries. And of course, my fellow British colleagues who in fact make up the majority of the NHS workforce.

It's been a pleasure working with you.

Acknowledgments

I would like to thank my daughters Elizabeth and Catherine for their support in helping me write this book as well as Dame Ruth Runciman, Prof Peter Tyrer, Sally Cunningham, Geraldine Cunningham, Madeline Marjoram, Sheila Gallagher and Melanie Hogan, who read earlier drafts and were helpful with their comments and suggestions.

Endorsements

Victoria Macdonald- Health and Social Care Editor, Channel 4 news:

Peter Carter's memoir, *My Asylum days* starts in the sixties, when he entered the system as a trainee psychiatric nurse. He says himself it was like stepping back in time. While drugs may have improved the treatment of people with severe mental illness, the conditions and the care were firmly rooted in the Victorian asylums. Dr Carter takes us on a journey through the following decades, as changes began to community. His book is made more powerful by the sensitive portrait he paints of the patients and his desire to make a difference. But it reminds us, too, that mental health still does not have parity with physical health and that no matter how far we have come there is still a long way to go.

Marjorie Wallace-Chief Executive, SANE:

"Dr Peter Carter's account weaves his own life and career from trainee psychiatric nurse to chief executive of the Royal College of Nursing with stories of the patients in his care over the past six decades.

He paints a poignant tableau of the old asylums: the often-shocking conditions of back wards in overcrowded institutions, as well as extraordinary acts of tenderness and compassion by dedicated doctors and nurses.

"It was only the vision of people like Dr Carter - together with the development of more effective medication - which led to a more enlightened approach to mental illness. But as he describes, the devastating impact of the wholescale closure of these hospitals, and the failed promises of care in the community to replace them, means that instead of liberating patients, many are still left at risk of neglect and suicide.

"This is essential reading for anyone interested in the history of mental illness, so that lessons can be learnt, and hope offered, of more responsive and effective care for people who, through no fault of their own, experience mental distress and despair."

Peter Tyrer – Emeritus Professor, Imperial College, London:

"It takes little thought to understand that mental health services are now under severe stress. But optimism is not absent".

"This book, written by (a giant in the field) Peter Carter, a former CEO of the Royal College of Nursing, examines the recent history of these services through a personal story – a story which shows great depth of understanding, compassion and humility; one which transcends the empty official orthodoxies which currently compete for our souls. Read it and grow".

Dr Dame Clare Gerada – Former President Royal College of General Practitioners:

"As a medical student, my psychiatric placement was at High Royds Asylum in the north of England. A vast mental hospital, equipped with sports facilities, a chapel and vast corridors, where patients seemingly paced around aimlessly all day (one only walked backwards). When later a trainee in psychiatry at the Maudsley hospital; I was sent to Cane Hill in South London. Again, a vast place which even had an on-site cemetery.

"Asylums were designed to be places of safety, where individuals could be housed and treated. Instead, however they seemed to be places where patients were "parked", often for decades, and where treatment seemed to be minimal. Therefore, Peter's book is so important. He lays bare the view that old mental hospitals should be condemned as nothing more than cruel institutions. His account, drawn from his lifetime in nursing (as a clinician, a manager and in later years, a leader) gives another view, as he describes with warmth and humour and honesty his experiences of caring for some of the most disadvantaged and unwell patients in society, whose lives were improved by the care they received in these institutions. Peter's book is a tour-de-force, as he traces the history of asylums from their inception to closure in the mid 1990's".

Printed in Great Britain
by Amazon

43270134R00136